Illuminating the Stories that Bind Us

*

*Breaking Through the Stories Between You,
Your Dreams, and Your Fully Expressed Life
of Joy and Bliss*

Jennifer H. Carey, Ed.S, LMHC

Dear Cousin
Cindy,
May this book help
illuminate and transform
any story (ies) that stand
between you and your
full expression of
joy and bliss.
Shine Unapologetically,
Jen Carey

Cover Design by Noah Stevens

Interior Design by Kate Reingold

ISBN: 9798335220859 (paperback edition)

*"I started to be free when I discovered
that the cage was made of thoughts."*
~ Author Unknown

This book is dedicated to my family of origin, also known as the family I was born into and raised by for most of my formative years: Mom, Kevin, Darlene, Dan, and Amber. I am who I am because of you, and I love who I am. My kindness, caring nature (CARE-Y—that's my last name!), creativity, sense of humor, and spirituality all began from the loving foundation you gave me and the unique qualities each of you possess. My livelihood as a psychotherapist came from my family, who were my first clients (wink).

No, seriously, thank you.

Please remember, dear family, as you read this, these are my stories. Our family's roles, dynamics, and patterns helped fuel the stories, but ultimately, my mind habitually projected the stories onto you and me. So, please read this in love and compassion for those stories. I share them here to help others.

My dream would be for us to break through these stories individually and as a family so we can live to our fullest potential individually and collectively as a unified, loving unit. It's already happening.

With love and gratitude,

Your daughter, your sister, your aunt

P.S. Though Dad left this earthly plane in 2012, he has lived on through every dream I have realized, including this book. I love you, Dad. You are in my mind and my soul forever.

Key

These are some helpful elements in this book:

Notes Page: On the last page of this book, you will find a note-taking page inspired both by my need to have visual aids and Brené Brown who spoke of it in her book, *Gifts of Imperfection*. Check that out first as you can use it as a tool as soon as you begin reading.

Journal Prompts: You will find journal prompts throughout this book that will help guide you on this journey of illumination and transformation.

Song Prescription: Whenever you see this symbol ♫ it signals the song that was prescribed by music coaches Mick and Tess Pulver of Breakthrough Performance Workshop.

Worksheets: There are helpful worksheets dispersed throughout this book to help you begin the process of illumination and transformation.

Parts Guide: This book uses many references to a powerful therapeutic approach called Internal Family Systems. The founder, Dr. Richard Schwartz, created this style of therapy as a tool to help us become more self-aware, self-connected, and empowered by knowing and understanding various aspects, or as he calls them, "Parts" of ourselves.

The premise is that we all have various Parts of ourselves born out of our family of origin or traumatic experiences. These Parts come alive to protect or manage our mental, emotional, and social functioning. Examples of these Parts include Perfectionism, Criticism, Anxiety, and Depression.

Our journey towards empowerment begins when we learn to detach from these Parts, thereby preventing them from dictating our lives. In this book, I adopt a personification and separation approach to help you gain perspective and distance from the narratives that bind you. Whenever I mention one of these Parts, I will capitalize it for clarity. I delve into this approach in Chapter 2, and there's a comprehensive Parts and Definitions section at the end of the book for a more detailed understanding of the various Parts.

Helpers: You will find references to therapists, coaches, healers and others who have helped me illuminate and break free from my stories. All of their contact information is at the end of this book.

An Invitation *for* You

Dear (*insert your name here*),

If you are anything like me, you have had various dreams throughout your life. My guess is that they started when you were a young child. Dreams that knock at your heart. Dreams that when you simply think of them, bring a sense of joy and hope.

At various points, you, like me, may have found that you were blocked or felt stuck on the path toward your dreams. No matter how much you knew what you really and truly wanted, you could not get out of your own way and take steps toward making it happen.

Would you believe me if I told you that the block you are bumping up against is a false story? And would you believe that this limiting belief (one that isn't even true!) is what is holding you back?

By taking the time to read this book, interact with the text, explore your inner world through the journal prompts and worksheets, and examine whatever block or obstacle to your dream is, you will discover that the very thing that is binding you is, in fact, a fiction story. And this book is meant to help you shine light upon, illuminate and transform the stories between you and your dreams.

If you are feeling skeptical about anything I have told you in this letter, that is completely normal.

We all have a Skeptic Part. The Part of us that questions or doubts opinions or viewpoints.

Please let your Skeptic Part know that you can see how it is trying to protect you somehow. Your Skeptic Part's intention is to doubt the theory I am proposing so you can stop before you start. That way, you stop before you potentially 'fail' on the way to your dreams. We can honor your Skeptic Part's intention in trying to protect you while at the same time not letting it lead your life.

Reader, I need you to know the true story: YOU ARE A STAR with the capacity to heal, learn, and grow through your limited stories so you can do what you are here to do: *shine*.

I am on a mission to help you know and live your dreams, express yourself fully, and fill your life with as much joy and flow as possible. So, Skeptic Parts of my dear readers, please step aside and allow these readers the opportunity to connect to this book and heal, learn, grow, connect, and realize their dreams.

With love and sincerity,

Jen

> **Journal Prompt:** What is a dream you have always held? Maybe you have had it since you were a child. Whenever this dream knocked on your heart, you knew that if you could live this dream in your lifetime, you would be stepping toward a fully expressed life. Write it down here, and let it be your compass. No matter what twists and turns you encounter, keep this as your North Star before, during and after reading this book.

Table of Contents

I share what brought me to this book, and when I knew it was time for me to illuminate and transform my stories. I also introduce the various healers, coaches, teachers and guides who have helped me along the way. You can find their info at the back of the book as well.

This chapter highlights stories from my podcast, *Illuminating the Stories that Bind Us*. Courageous participants get vulnerable and share a story that is binding them. Within each story is a checklist of ways the story may show up, a song prescribed to help break through that specific story, and a journal prompt to deepen your awareness of limiting beliefs in your own life. There's a bonus section on holding dichotomies that you won't want to miss.

Have I told you lately that I love PARTS WORK?! This chapter explores the incredible work of Dr. Richard Schwartz and how our self-awareness and self-connection can deepen even more when we think about a certain Part of us holding specific stories. There's also a journal prompt to help you explore your own inner world.

There are general guideposts that help set the stage to do this inner work based on qualities like curiosity, non-judgment and compassion. Learn more on how best to lay the groundwork before your inner journey begins. Also included in this chapter is a worksheet that will help you illuminate a story that is binding you.

Read about real-life examples where stories that we hold and we project onto our relationships can stunt your growth and joy. The "Layers of Stories Technique" is outlined with an accompanying step by step worksheet and samples that can be used with yourself, a partner, a friend, or a family member to make sure a story does not create a casualty out of a healthy and important relationship. Journal prompts are included in this one too. Frequently Asked Questions are given here to help you when you use this technique, and to know when it is better *not* to use it.

Chapter 5: Stories from Others, Stories We Give Others

Gossip. Messaging. Projection. How do we become more aware of the stories that others have projected onto us and the ones we've put on other people. There's a journal prompt to help deepen this awareness and the beloved hack from Brene Brown: Story in My Head.

Chapter 6: The Importance of Illuminating the Stories that Bind Us

Learn about my real-life nudges, a.k.a wake-up calls that directed me onto the illumination path. Also, this chapter has a checklist to see if you are being nudged. I reference coaches and healers again here; you can find their contact info in the Appendix. There's a journal prompt and a check-in quiz to ensure you are clear about the nudges you may or may not be receiving.

Chapter 7: Rewards of Illuminating and Transforming Our Stories

Learn about the amazing and powerful rewards I have experienced from doing the work of illuminating my stories. These examples will keep you going and show how it improved my relationships, career path, creative outlets, and hobbies.

Chapter 8: Obstacles While Illuminating and Transforming Our Stories

It's inevitable. When we begin to do this work and step toward our goals and dreams, we are going to bump up against challenges and obstacles. I describe ones that I have faced or have witnessed others face. Don't worry. For every obstacle, I include a Shift Tip or a tool that will help you navigate and move beyond the obstacle. I even include Shift Tips for fears your Resistant Parts may be holding. There's a journal prompt and a moment to pause, reflect and regroup before moving on to the next phase of this work.

PART 2: TRANSFORMING THE STORIES

It is one thing to illuminate. After you shed light on the stories, then it is time to take the action needed to dissolve them so that you can step into your dreams and your fullest potential. Beginning with your dream or goal itself, this section gives you a roadmap that can guide you through breaking through stories and achieving your desires. I call this roadmap the *Divine Dream Dance*.

Chapter 9: Defining Our Dreams and the Roadmap to Get There

Use a chart to really understand what I mean when I say, "Divine Dream Dance."

Chapters 10-15: Divine Dream Dance, Stages 1-6

Each stage of the dream is described through quotes, descriptions and personal examples from my experience with these stages when I was accomplishing one of my biggest dreams in this life. More tools and interventions as well as journal prompts provided give you an opportunity to tap into your dreams and creative forces to make them a reality.

Chapter 16: The Opportunity and Space for You to Transform

Learn how the power of creative, expressive and performing arts is backed by history and brain science. Become more aware of the stories that stand between us and these transformative tools. Commit to becoming more aware of how you can use these tools to help you break through your limiting beliefs and false narrative and experience more joy and bliss, creativity, freedom, and connection.

Acknowledgments

Welcome

In this section, I share what prompted me to write this book and refer to the coaches, healers, guides, and colleagues who have helped me along the way. Their contact information is at the end of the book.

I can still recall the session with my client when the seed of the idea for this book was watered. Picture this: my client and I are in a small office, sitting across from each other. I know and see a caring, sensitive, witty, and intelligent man. He can spur an out-loud gut-belly laugh at least once or twice a session. He consistently wins Employee of the Year. He tried to quit his job repeatedly, but every time he left, they bribed him with more money to come back.

All of this is true. Yet. Yet! This client came in week after week with symptoms of angst, anxiety, and low self-worth. He would express stories that he carried in his head: stories that his manager and employers think he is garbage, stories that nobody likes him, and fearful thoughts that someday they would find out he is a fraud.

His narratives did not match my experience in his presence and the rewards and accolades he reported receiving at work. To this day, I tease this client and say: "Someday, I will do a documentary where I go and interview all of your colleagues. Then I'll play the interviews back to you and see what happens to your stories when they come up against something different."

That is the moment it dawned on me, and the seed of this book sprouted. Many of my clients came in with stories like this. My friends and family share stories of what other people think of them and what they think of themselves, too. Are all of these stories incongruent with what happened, similar to how the facts didn't match my clients' stories above?

My realization with this client inspired me to look closer at myself. I realized I had similar stories, especially those related to my family of origin. (Note how I used the past tense—had—because (spoiler alert!) the stories have dissolved with only a hint of them left. Keep reading this book to see how you can dissolve yours, too (wink, wink)).

When I took a closer look at myself and those around me, I noticed more and more how most of us in this human experience carry stories around in our heads as if they were facts. Sometimes, these stories can be small and created in an instant. For example, a person in the grocery store gives you a dirty look, and you immediately interpret it into a story that they are judging your weight or appearance. Other times, our stories are more significant and come from what authority figures told us as children, which we then translate into fact. Messages, such as, "You will never amount to anything." We can also create stories out of a traumatic experience or family dynamic, such as, **"I was not able to fix my family after that crisis, so I will never be enough and therefore have to try my hardest to exist and make up for what I was not able to do for my family."** I had an inkling that the latter was the story or belief that I was carrying. All of these wonderings needed deeper illumination.

These informal findings motivated me to try my own experiment to see if any of the conclusions were valid. My hypothesis for this experiment was that we carry around stories that we believe are true but are in fact, false. These inaccurate beliefs that we begin to live by can cause us anxiety and depression and hold us back from experiencing more joy, bliss, and connection in our relationships. My method of testing its validity was to have a trusted facilitator interview me and my siblings separately, first having me share what I thought each of my siblings thought of me and then asking each of my siblings individually what they thought of me (without knowing the stories I shared). Note: Only one sibling agreed to participate, my oldest brother.

This is how the experiment went: We recorded everything visually and audibly over Zoom.

First, my dear colleague Dayna Wood of Integrative Counsel interviewed me and asked two main questions:

Describe your relationships with your siblings and what you believe they think of you. In other words, what story do you live out day by day thinking they think of you and how those beliefs impact you.

What do you wish for them to know about you, and what do you want for them and your relationships?

Then she asked my oldest brother these central questions:

Describe your relationship with Jen.

What do you think of Jen? How would you describe her as a person, a sister?

What do you wish for her to know? What wisdom do you have for her to help her step into her power?

The last step of this process was Dayna, my oldest brother and I all watching the interviews together and seeing whether or not my story matched what he thought of me.

Through tears during our first meeting with just Dayna and me, I shared my interpretation of what each of my siblings thought of me. Essentially, the stories I carried were: **"I need to make everything okay and make sure everyone in my family is fine, and if I fall short, well then, I am nothing, and I have failed. If I cannot go above and beyond to help fix their problems and help them feel better, I'm abandoning them and therefore unlovable."**

Talk about pressure.

In the interview with Dayna, we realized that I carried multiple stories, and another story that came up was about feeling like I was a "Golden Child" for my parents because I was such an "easy child." From that interpretation, I believed **I need NOT SHINE anymore and take any light away from my siblings**. In the interview, I also expressed the answer to the second question, my wish: that I could rewrite this dynamic and show up as me in this family without this pressure. I wished that we could all coexist, perfectly imperfect, with no expectations that I would need to care for everyone else and make everything better. I wanted to shine naturally and be fully me, allowing my siblings to do the same. Before this experiment, I did not know how much power there was in transforming these beliefs through these interviews alone. This part of the process, alone, was enlightening.

In the interview with my brother, he described me as "perfect," always there for everyone. And his wish for me was for me to know that he appreciated everything about me, everything about my personality and that I was the reason he was still alive. It was quite different from the "not enough" story I had held in my head. This confirmed my hypothesis and what I would believe would happen if we interviewed the client's colleagues at the beginning of this section.

There are so many gems to take away from this experiment.

The first gem is the power of illumination. Simply having the safe space to share what I thought my family thought of me made me more aware than I had ever been of what stories I was carrying around that were causing unnecessary weight and pressure.

The second gem is that we often carry more than one story.

The third gem is that we often carry stories that are beyond human capacity. In other words, we expect things about ourselves that are way beyond what we can do in human form and often beyond what we can influence in someone else's life or journey.

The fourth gem came with realizing that I held the key to transforming these stories. True, it was revealing and validating to have my brother's input recorded to prove that at least one of my siblings did not carry the same story that I did. My brother did not hold the thoughts about me that I had assumed. He did not think that I was "not enough" or "unloveable". And now that I have that evidence, it is on me to do the inside work to heal this story I have lived under for so long. I have been putting the pressure of these stories and expectations on myself. Therefore, it is on me and in my power to transform them.

The last but most important gem is that underneath everything was love. Dayna so beautifully reflected that at one point. Underneath the stories, the seemingly fixed roles in the family is love. Family dynamics and relationships can be like a landmine, but at the core, there is *love*. So, we must dig through the stories that are not real to reach that core of love.

There was a point at the very end of the experiment where my brother was concerned that my breaking through my story would change my role in my family. And that part did not feel good or okay with him. That worried him. Quite frankly, I think that worries many people when illuminating their stories. In the section on the challenges of illuminating, I speak more about what stops people from making these constructive and positive changes. My hope is that people will be aware of their hesitations in illuminating and still continue to learn the benefits of life on the other side. Illuminating the stories that bind us is well worth the journey.

The most important lesson that I took from this experiment is this: **without awareness or illumination of these stories, I would carry on with the false belief that I'm either not enough OR that I need not shine and take away the light from others. Not fact. We must start by becoming more aware of our stories. Otherwise, we can live out those stories even if they are proven not to be true and wind up shrinking, freezing or expanding accordingly.** It is my mission to take the tagline that I've had since 2008: "to help myself and others heal, learn and grow" and help you become gently mindful of your own stories so that you can be empowered and in control of your life rather than allowing your limiting stories having complete control and power.

Inspired by the findings before and after the experiment with Dayna, I began my podcast, *Illuminating the Stories that Bind Us*, where brave and courageous participants share a story that is binding them as a way to become more aware of their limiting story and for others to be able to hear it and potentially relate and heal, learn and grow alongside them. Then, at the end of the podcast, music coaches Mick and Tess Pulver of Breakthrough Performance Workshop prescribed a song that helps the participant transform that story. Awareness is the first step and 50% of the solution. Once you have the awareness, then it is time to transform the story. The song and music helps transform the false story and help shift to a positive and more empowering narrative.

In this book, I will take you on the rest of my journey of illuminating and transforming my personal stories, as well as share the stories of other brave and courageous participants that many of us can relate to. There are sections to help you become self-aware and others to help improve your relationships. I include many tools to help you learn how to navigate your limiting beliefs and false stories so they do not rule your life. At the end of the book, you learn about navigating your own dance with your dreams so your stories do not hold you back from achieving them. In this next section we begin this process with learning about the stories shared on my podcast. You will have the opportunity to see if you can relate to any of their stories.

Let us see.

PART I

Illuminating the Stories

Chapter I

✳

Seven Common Stories that Bind Us

The stories highlighted in this chapter were pulled from my podcast, *Illuminating the Stories that Bind Us*, in which courageous participants get vulnerable and share a story that is binding them. For each story, I include a checklist of ways the false belief may appear in your life. I encourage you to gently and curiously move through these stories, holding compassion for the person who shared it and compassion toward yourself and anyone else you know who may carry it. At the end of each story, there is a journal prompt that you can use to help you heal and process how you relate to the story. Then, as mentioned in the section above, each participant receives a song prescribed by Mick and Tess Pulver to help transform the story.

 If you wish to listen to any of these episodes, you can find them at www.jenniferhcarey.com/podcasts

Okay. It's time. Together, let's illuminate and break through the stories that are binding us.

The story I'm about to illuminate for you is truly the impetus for this book.

As I write this, I am grateful for illuminating it and working through many layers of healing, and at the same time, I'm amazed at how I continue to bump into new layers around this. The good news is that I am changed, and this story does not have nearly the hold on me that it did when I first started the illumination journey.

STORY #1

I'm not enough for my family.

"Being enough was going to have to be an inside job."
~ Anne Lamott

Here's a quick checklist with some of the ways this story can come up in your life:

You or someone you know may:

- ☐ Feel anxious around family and feel a desperate need to make everything okay for them
- ☐ Experience a steady stream of guilt that you need to do more
- ☐ Carry a fear of disappointing your family
- ☐ Have a low sense of worth that you are just never enough and you keep missing the mark
- ☐ Worry about hurting other people's feelings

Can you relate to this story or know someone who can?

First, I want to share an excerpt from the incredible book, *The Choice*, by psychologist Dr. Edith Eva Eger, a woman who survived the Holocaust. She writes of something we should all think about within our family system:

> I came along, and there was already a complete family. They had a daughter who played piano and a daughter who played violin. I am unnecessary. I am not good enough. There is no room for me, I think.

Dr. Eger further says: "This is the way we misinterpret the facts of our lives.

The way we assume and don't check it out. The way we invent a story to tell ourselves. Reinforcing the very thing in us, we already believe."

Like the author, I was born into an already-operating family. My identity was definitely formed around being the family mediator/therapist/savior. I can't remember exactly when it started. I do know, however, that I always felt like I had to maintain all of the relationships in my family as best I could. This "role" started very young.

One of the common statements my mom would say to me, which she was likely not aware of, was: "Talk to _____ (insert family member) and fix things, and make it better." Now, "make it better" could mean to help make the specific family member feel better, help fix their problems, or help mend their relationship with my mom, or all of the above. I remember, at an early age, my mom wished I would fix her relationship with her mother or her sister. She wanted me to fix the relational things that were not going well within our family. "Talk to your brother." "Talk to your sister." Little did she know that a constellation of inner parts was being formed.

You may recall in "The Key," I speak to Internal Family Systems (IFS) and Parts Work at the start of this book. Parts Work is a central element of my work as a therapist as well as my own personal healing journey. The language, understanding, and tools of Parts Work help make sense of the stories that bind us, so you will find it used throughout this book. I go into further detail about IFS and Parts Work in the next section of this chapter. I capitalize the Parts to help signify that I am writing about a specific Part. The messaging described above from my mom to me as a child, created a Fixer Part that would reside within me. This Part has many gifts, as our Parts often do. However, when my Fixer Part is working to an extreme, I experience anxious symptoms around fearing I won't be able to fix or solve something. In addition to a Fixer Part, a People Pleaser would go above and beyond to try and make things okay, overwhelming me with dread and guilt when it feels like I have not done that. These Parts and their extreme expectations would stay stuck in this pattern and carry stories for many years, until I started to reprogram them.

What became and continues to be the most difficult realization for me was that I could NOT and can NOT fix others. While I do believe I can help make things better just by my positivity, helpfulness, natural skillset and generally good nature, I've come to grasp this startling conclusion: I cannot fix what is someone else's journey… and most things are someone else's journey, and outside of my control.

Herein lies my story. The story that I am not enough for my family was developed because in actuality I could never be "ENOUGH" for them. The ability to fix or solve their situation is ultimately in their hands. They hold the key to the betterment of their lives. It is fascinating that, even as I write this, I am still attempting to convince the cells of my body that this is the case. Somehow, I got it in my head that I was supposed to fix them and their situations—and if I didn't, who was I? And worse yet—if I couldn't, was I even loveable?

What this turned into over time was a lot of guilt and self-esteem issues. It also presented itself as incredible anxiety. Many of these symptoms have improved a million times through my journey of illuminating and transforming this story. Once in a while, when I'm with my family—especially if they are facing a problem or crisis —there is still a whisper that plays in my head: "Ready, set, go, Jen: please everyone, help everyone, spend time with everyone, FIX everything, make it better or else you will not be loveable." Now, I know what this is when it happens, and I can better discern my role in the family with clarity and healthy boundaries.

An important stage of my illumination journey with this "not enough for my family" story, was when I checked it out with one of my brothers, as you read about earlier. My brother assured me of how loved and adored I was. That helped with my "unlovable" story for sure. In that process, we also saw clearly how I had this sense of responsibility underneath the Fixer Part, and we both panicked a bit knowing this role and story no longer served me. There was a quiet knowing that this would need to shift in order for me to feel more peace. And when it came to reassigning my role as Fixer, we both panicked. He panicked thinking of the unknown: "What happens if Jen is no longer the "mother figure" or "helper" in our family?" I panicked, too, because of the old fear that if this part of me stepped back, I would not be loved. I remember assuring him (and myself) that was not the goal. Which is somewhat true. I will always be the helpful, kind, caring, loving, compassionate daughter/sister/aunt, but I will no longer cling to the idea that if I do not fix or save, I am worthless. That was the story in my head that had been most damaging. And since it was inside MY OWN HEAD where this binding story lived, I realized that unbinding would be an INSIDE JOB. It is on me to do the inner work.

In the podcast episode of this story, music coaches Mick and Tess Pulver prescribed me the song, "Right to be Wrong" by Joss Stone.

My journey with this song feels somewhat eternal. From the moment they prescribed it to me and I practiced it after the podcast, until I sang it *live* in front of an audience, I felt the power of the lyrics and emotion that Joss Stone gives it in her gift of song. The stanza that hit me square in the eyes the first time I heard it was this:

"You're entitled to your opinion, but it's really my decision, I can't turn back, I'm on a mission, if you care, don't you dare, blur my vision: LET ME BE ALL THAT I CAN BE—Don't smother me with negativity."

Those lyrics resonate because my pattern of being unlovable unless I could fix/save was holding me back in so many ways. I was stuck in a feedback pattern of not being good enough…which I'm breaking free of while hoping to help others that share this story and pattern, to break through too.

I still sing that song with so much emotion and conviction. It gives me the space to be who I am, and helps me to be unafraid of not being "the everything" that I perceive other people expect me to be. I performed it with an acoustic guitar and live audience in May of 2022 as the kickoff to the first WOW Retreat. I shared this story with the audience and then was able to belt it out in front of them. If you would like to see it live, you can see it on my YouTube channel at: *https://www.youtube.com/@heallearngrow*

Around the time I was illuminating my stories and working with music coaches to transform them, I worked with an Internal Family Systems therapist to help support me and my Parts throughout this journey. When she told me she was retiring, I did a review of all of our work together. When I came to this story, I realized that the charge of this story was nearly gone. So, this journey with therapy, life coaching, musical coaching, shamanic healing and performing arts had truly worked its powers. At one time, I can honestly say that this story led me and how I functioned in relationships. This story has much less of a hold on me now. Without this story running the show, I feel freer, happier, more relaxed and less anxious to fix what I cannot fix. Furthermore, it brings me closer to my family, because the walls of fear between us are dissolving. That is how powerful these stories can be.

Another perspective that has helped break through these stories is that there isn't something to fix. In other words, who am I to say someone needs "fixing." More and more, I have been able to pause and remind myself that everyone has their journey in this life. Unless they openly ask me to help them navigate something or assist them in making positive changes, I need to stay in my lane, focus on myself, and work on my journey.

Poem and Journal Prompt

Poetry and journaling can also be powerful tools to transform our stories. Please incorporate poetry and journaling to help yourself in this process of illumination and transformation. You can see here how it helped me move through temporary pain so that I could experience freedom.

I wrote this poem at a beach in Beverly, Massachusetts, after I had decided not to go to my hometown for the weekend. I knew I was disappointing my family, and the guilt was gut-wrenching. I had wanted to stay close to home, though. Enjoy the summer. Relax. Restore. And I felt so selfish and torn for making that decision, though everything in my body had told me, *stay home, take care of yourself.* I was beginning to listen to my own needs over my family's needs. This still feels uncomfortable sometimes, yet it's what is needed for my evolution.

In the midst of my turmoil, I wrote this:

Do Snakes Feel Pain When They Shed Their Skin?

As I shed a story and belief that has been a part of my identity since I was a child, I feel this thick layer of pain across my heart and my gut.

I look down as what no longer serves me sheds bit by bit. I wiggle to help it shed so the pain and discomfort lessens.

Who am I without this skin? Will people still recognize me? Will people still love and adore me?

Will I still have a place in my family? Will friends still want to be my friend? Will I still have a place in this world?

Who am I without this skin?

When I listen to what my body is telling me,

I know I'm lighter and can give more light.

I know I'm freer and can roam more land.

I know I have more energy and can heal more people.

I know I can feel the ground more easily and can expand my heart with more reach.

Do snakes feel pain when they shed their skin? And if so, how long does it last?

Journal Prompt: Do you have a story you inherited from your family of origin that no longer serves you? Is that story a layer of skin you can shed? Name that layer of skin you would like to shed and to the best of your ability, describe the various feelings of shedding that layer.

STORY #2

I am bad and deserve to be punished.

"When we hold secrets it creates shame, and shame is a great barrier to success. When you carry the shame you do not allow yourself to fulfill your greatest potential, you do not honor the truth of yourself, you do not honor your highest self. When you let go of the secret, only then you live to your greatest potential."
~ Oprah Winfrey

Here's a quick checklist with some of the ways this story can come up in your life:

You or someone you know may:

- ☐ Notice patterns of self-sabotage in relationships, career, and other life goals
- ☐ Are constantly in fear that you are going to get caught for something you didn't even do or that didn't even happen
- ☐ Feel the need to constantly be on the defense
- ☐ Feel stuck and cannot move forward on your dreams
- ☐ Struggle to follow through and maintain the things that you know are good for you

Can you relate to this story or know someone who can?

Let us turn to a story from someone other than me. The story, "I am bad and deserve to be punished," is more common than we realize. Thanks to the courageous participant in this episode, it is being brought to light so that everyone who can relate can be unbound.

This brave participant had all of the above patterns in the checklist show up in her life. I remember being struck by how much healing work she had done to understand the pieces of when and how this story began which you will read about below. She also shared wisdom for those who do not know how this story began. This participant had some significant shifts after we did the podcast. I will share more about all of this a little later, too.

For readers who can identify when or how this story may have begun, please greet it with gentle curiosity and compassion. You may know exactly where it came from because of the punishment and abuse that you experienced. This may be triggering, and I encourage you to give yourself what I would provide for you if I had the honor of having you in my healing space: unconditional love, acceptance, and non-judgment. Please keep a neutral and observant stance, knowing that the courage of this awareness will pay dividends in your healing process.

People who can relate to this story may carry it without any history of abuse. However, many people can correlate this story to an experience of physical, sexual, or emotional abuse. For that reason, a portion of this section will help us understand the complex layers of this story when trauma and abuse are the cause of this story. Those who can relate to this story may be able to recall from childhood an experience where there was abuse or an assault of some kind. Perhaps it was a pattern or a one-time event. Whether the abuse was emotional, physical, or sexual, it can leave you with the residue of feeling like you did something wrong, even when you did not. This residue can feel full of contradictions: strong yet hidden, pleasant yet unpleasant, memorable yet dissociative. A survival technique often used when abuse has occurred is to bury the shame story or experience deep within the subconscious. But it's still there. "Our issues are in our tissues," so our body remembers, but the brain may be unable to identify it and differentiate that "this was not your fault."

Furthermore, when we are children, our identity and brain are still forming, and we look to authority figures to help guide us and give us a compass. Whatever an authority figure tells us is impressionable. An adult's messaging and a gut feeling can be conflicting and confusing for a child. You may or may not know that children always aim to please, love, and be loved. For example, physical touch can make one feel good physically and emotionally. There are nerve fibers in our skin that send signals of pleasure and connection when we experience touch. Not to mention, receiving any attention from an adult feels good, too. The innocence and desire to connect that is innate in children can make what an adult says and does challenging to navigate. Mixed messages can be super confusing. That is often where these stories begin. Children will take responsibility for things they can't control or fix and are not their responsibility. Illuminating the story around this healing revelation is vital. Otherwise, the story will keep coming out in ways we need help understanding.

Let me explain this with examples and scenarios that help illuminate this further.

- A young child is emotionally and physically abused throughout their life and finds themself as an adult pushing buttons, looking for a way to bring on the anger and abuse that was their familiar environment; that is all they know.
- A sexually-abused child is confused because the touch they experienced felt good to them physically. However, socially, something does not feel right, and that is reinforced by societal messages around shame and sex. Intuitively, something does not feel right because there is this conflicting feeling in their gut. The perpetrator is telling them they will punish the child if they tell anyone. This confusion can/will follow them and leave them always holding a story of shame and fear of being punished.
- A young adult is sexually assaulted and told by the perpetrator that it was the clothes they were wearing and the way they flirted that caused the perpetrator to do it. Suddenly, the young adult believes it is their fault, and they deserve to be punished.

I could go on, but hopefully, you understand, and your compassion for yourself and others with this story is building.

The participant in this episode remembers running down the stairs at the age of 4 and telling her mother that she needed to be punished, but neither her mother nor she knew why. She also shares how this story of being punished became a self-fulfilling prophecy, and she began telling herself, "See, you are bad!" at every slight mistake she made.

Our participant shares a profound insight that has resonated with many of our listeners: "It's okay if you don't know why you feel this way." This simple yet powerful statement has been a source of healing for many, as they realized they didn't need to force understanding. They discovered the strength in their own unique story, with all its power and magic. If the source of their pain is hidden, it may be a natural trauma response, a survival technique to protect them from unbearable pain.

This participant leaves these words in relation to her story: **"It's okay if it never goes away, what's important is how I show up for that part of me."** Let those words inspire you as you show up to your own stories. They may still be there, even if they are faint. How you respond to it matters. Show up in the same way you would show up to a wounded or hurt child. Show up with compassion, presence, understanding and watch it continue to heal.

🎵 Music coaches Mick and Tess Pulver prescribed the song "Perfect" by Pink. They shared that you are perfect no matter what and how when you open to the healing message of this song, you can cut through and break through many hard things. The client was excited to work with the song stating: "Pink is a powerhouse and I am too . . . when I am not paralyzed."

Please go listen to this song, or another song that helps you feel loved and empowered, and sing it to yourself in the mirror—everyone needs to do that.

Follow up

I was fortunate to do a few follow-up podcasts with participants a few months after they had illuminated their story for us all. What happened to this participant afterwards is mind blowing. Here are her follow-up reflections and shocking experience:

> Going into this I did not expect—I thought it would be helpful just to talk about things—I was shocked by some things that transpired after the session that seemed directly connected. The interview was on a Friday, and the next morning—a family member called and told me about a dream and the dream was directly related to content shared in the podcast and the podcast had not been broadcast yet and this family member had NO IDEA about this podcast. Then, because of that sharing, it turned into a very healing and transformative conversation. We talked about dynamics in a brand-new way. To have a new way to talk about it and have the person take some ownership and responsibility of some things they had done was amazing and at the same time took time to process and integrate because it was so new. The script was changed. Change can happen at any stage and to not give up hope. A constructive conversation that people dream about having can happen."

Mission accomplished—the ripple effects of illuminating the story that binds us. I was deeply moved that this happened as a result of our conversation. And I was further honored that the participant shared that the gentle tone used in our conversation on the podcast had carried over into her conversation with her family member. This opened up a new softness in how she and her family member communicated going forward.

The biggest take away is to share your story. Sharing your story will change you and will change those around you too, including family and loved ones.

Final Notes on This Significant Topic

Whether the source of the story is memorable or not, my wish for you who are trapped by it is that you will liberate yourself by:

- Bringing the story to light and awareness.

- Giving yourself permission to forgive yourself for carrying it.
- Knowing that you are the only one who can be you, and you are worthy of stepping into your fullest potential at work, in your relationships, and in your dreams.
- Believing in yourself and knowing that YOU are a star just by being you.
- Remember, you are the author of your life. Not the story. Not the Saboteur Part.
- Rewrite your story. The pen is in your hands.

Journal prompt: Have you ever punished yourself by replaying a story in a way that was not loving? If yes, describe that story here with gentle curiosity and compassion.

STORY #3

The reason he doesn't love me anymore is because I'm not _____(pretty, intelligent, rich. . .) enough.

"When we lose a relationship, the stories we associate with the loss seem to break our hearts far more than the grief itself."
~ Jennifer H. Carey

Here's a quick checklist with some of the ways this story can come up in your life:

You or someone you know may:

- ☐ Find yourself obsessing after a breakup over all the possible reasons and moments you turned off a lover and they turned away
- ☐ Struggle to try and figure out what behavior will be the most appealing—expressing love or playing hard to get
- ☐ Cling to the past or what could have been instead of the present and reality
- ☐ Feel less confident dating
- ☐ Guard your heart and seek emotionally unavailable partners

Can you relate to this story or know someone who can?

The stories we hold in our heads after losing a relationship are intense. In Episode 3 of my podcast, I share a true and juicy story that occurred when I had a strong connection with a flamenco guitarist in Spain while studying Spanish and Flamenco dance. The context for a fairy tale or a Hallmark Movie, heh? The connection was one of those twin flames, incredible connections in which you feel like you've known a person in a past life story. But that was not the story that bound me. The story that bound me was the reasons I projected onto why he ended it. On top of being long distance, our situation had many complications and layers to the story that made it so it was not meant to continue. Timing. Circumstances. That was the true story.

However, I created my own false story. My story was that I was not smart enough, worldly enough, didn't know enough Spanish (or any other language because he knew at least three), wasn't pretty enough, didn't know enough Flamenco... Fill in the blank to imply that I was not enough of something, and that was the story that I took and ran with, into a deep, dark hole.

I can look back and see how I projected this story onto every dating experience I had for at least a decade after that experience with him. When/if things did not work out with someone I connected with, I would fill it in with this "not enough" story.

This story did motivate me to go on an incredible mission of self-love. I read about self-love, and performed rituals and practices to enhance it, from love letters to myself to positive affirmations. That journey was priceless. And I am so grateful that by some Divine Intervention, the "not enough" stories didn't ambush my ability to see my value, open up and date, and eventually marry my husband. So, the story was healed and transformed by my healing and self-love work. Thank Goodness I made lemonade from the lemons of this experience!

However, what I have found most heartbreaking about this is I cannot tell you how many clients, friends, and relatives I witness having the same interpretation after a loss of love. One person's experience of not being ready for a relationship (timing and circumstances) causes a whole novel of how awful the person they broke up with is. I spend a lot of time trying to tell my clients that the breakup has more to do with their ex and where their ex is in life. I look at them and exclaim: "You are still a light, a prize; know this about yourself. Keep learning to love yourself more despite this breakup." I don't know if that message gets through their teary eyes and all the stories they hold in those tears, but I still try.

Fourteen years after this lost lover story was born, I had the priceless blessing of reconnecting with this man I met in Granada, Spain. We reconnected over the internet, and I asked him, "Why did you end things?" His response: "I was a mess, and you were an A+, and I knew I would mess things up with you, too."

The "not enough" story that my Wounded Part had carried for at least a decade was shattered in that one response. I was fortunate to share my story with him, and he was brave enough to admit his reason for cutting things off.

This whole experience became one of my biggest inspirations in following this mission. If I can help people illuminate these binding stories that come from falsely interpreting the loss of a relationship, I can spread a self-love revolution. So, pause right now and inventory your loss of love stories. If you find yourself coming up with a story full of self-judgment and self-destruction, consider the possibility that the story may have been more about timing and circumstances. The story could have been more about the person who ended things and where they were on their journey.

One public service announcement: if/when you decide to end a relationship, give that person enough information about your reasoning so that they do not create their own story in their head. The trend of ghosting has impacted people and left them confused. It is devastating. Let us put an end to that destruction. Many people ghost because they fear hurting someone else, but those people are just allowing their Coward Part to lead. Be brave. Be honest. Be constructive for both of you. I know it can be hard to articulate, so seek some help and support to do so, and you will prevent ripples of suffering. Thank you.

On that note, let me shift gears for a second here and speak to the flip side; if you were brave and honest and ended things with someone and you experienced shaming for your reasoning for ending the relationship, I highly recommend the following:

- Check with an aware and trusted friend or family member to sift through what could apply and what could not apply.
- Engage in therapy to filter out what lessons you could learn about yourself regarding being in a relationship. Learning and becoming more aware of yourself will also benefit you in future relationships.
- Remember that it is possible that the person you broke up with may be hurt and embarrassed and be showing you a shame response. In other words, they may be attacking you as a way to process their hurt and embarrassment. You can meet that Shame Part of them with compassion as they tend to their wound. Again, meeting with someone objective to assist you in filtering through the possible layers of stories and dynamics would be most helpful.

Moral of the story: Don't do this alone. Since many people in these situations end up internalizing the stories, blocking their hearts, and choosing never to date again, it is important you prevent that from happening. In relationships, we can always learn more about ourselves. Remember to take the time to get clear about what is on your side of the street and what is on their side of the street. Don't allow anyone to put their garbage on your side of the street, thinking that it's yours.

🎵 For this experience, music coaches Mick and Tess Pulver prescribed me the song, "That I Would Be Good" by Alanis Morrisette. The first time I tried to sing the song, I cried through the whole thing. The tears I cried were for me and everyone in the world carrying a "not enough" story. I wonder if Alanis knows how healing this song is. I sang this song at the Songbirds Cabaret at the first ever WOW Stage and shared the above story. You can check it out on my YouTube channel (*https://www.youtube.com/@heallearngrow*) or listen to Alanis and let her healing words and melody wash over and cleanse all of your fears around not being enough and trust that you will be good no matter what.

Journal Prompt: Do you have a "not enough" story from a loss of love? If yes, illuminate it here by writing it down. Next, step back, zoom out and describe how timing, circumstances and where the other person is/was may be the story or reason they ended things. Write about and consider that possibility too.

I am an imposter.

"It might surprise you to discover that some of the superstars you see on the big screen or those entertaining thousands in stadiums, have moments of sheer terror before they go on stage. They also compare themselves to others in their field and worry that they will not live up to the expectations of those who are supporting and depending on them."
~Trish Taylor

Here's a quick checklist with some of the ways this story can come up in your life:

You or someone you know may:

- ☐ Have difficulty receiving compliments because you do not believe they are true or about you
- ☐ Hold people at arm's length for fear that if they are too close, they will discover you are a fraud
- ☐ Experience low self-esteem and confidence
- ☐ Be constantly waiting for the other shoe to drop
- ☐ Have anxiety: from social to performance—because you do not believe in yourself

Can you relate to this story or know someone who can?

It's time to discuss something more common than you think: Imposter Syndrome. Studies have shown that 70% of leaders have this. Imposter syndrome is when you doubt your skills and talents and feel like someday people will find out that you are a fraud—that you are a fake, whether it is a fraud friend, fraud partner, fraud employee, etc.

The phrase "Fake it until you make it" supports this concept or story. The truth is that there are many times in our lives when we have to show up and "pretend we know" until we learn. Many of our first years at a new job are like this, and since we are always learning, this is a part of the process.

But what happens when this is your narrative? Suddenly, you doubt and question everything about yourself. You minimize gifts and talents and stop believing in yourself. It's heartbreaking.

In Season 1, Episode 15, entitled "I am an Imposter," a brave participant shares her story of feeling like an imposter. She shares how she is constantly anxious, worrying about when people will find out or the other shoe will drop.

For this participant, this story started when she was a quiet young girl and always felt anxious in social situations. She worked hard to push through the anxiety and to be social anyway. One of her coping mechanisms for her shyness was to pretend that she was not anxious and had a normal social life. She implemented the "Fake it until you make it" phrase, and this tool was helpful in moving her beyond the fear so she was able to connect with others.

However, for this participant, it was both a blessing and a curse because she then worried, "When will they realize that I'm not as cool as they think I am?"

Flash forward, and this has moved beyond friends and into her career and romantic relationship. It steals her joy and keeps her from fully embracing the love and accomplishment around her. Specifically, in her romantic relationship, she often compared herself to other women her boyfriend worked with or would talk to and was afraid she never measured up to them.

Fortunately, she has shared with me that this story and Imposter syndrome have gotten much lighter since the podcast, and she is getting more confident and enjoying her social life and career more. She feels like she is deserving and can be more present. She keeps a close eye on her Imposter and Comparison Parts and steps into her uniqueness, knowing she is the only one who CAN be her and is less intimidated and jealous of other women and her boyfriend.

♫ For this participant and her story, music coaches Mick and Tess prescribed a powerful song for her: "Like It or Not" by Madonna. Check out that song. I had never heard this song before this podcast. When I listened to it, I immediately put my shoulders back and pranced around with more confidence and assuredness in myself. My goodness, Mick and Tess are good at this!

Journal Prompt: How has imposter syndrome shown up in your life? If yes, make it into Imposter Part (a part of you) and write a compassionate letter thanking it for trying to protect you. Close your letter with: "Thank you for stepping back and allowing me to step forward and shine."

STORY #5

If you are financially abundant, you must be taking advantage of someone, so it's better to be selfless, help others and struggle financially.

"The number 1 money block is your family money legacy."
~ Sherold Barr

Here's a quick checklist with some of the ways this story can come up in your life:

You or someone you know may:

- ☐ Find it hard to accept money or charge money
- ☐ Connect your self-worth with money (e.g. if you do not think you're good enough or worthy of money, you may be less likely to request, accept or receive money, even when appropriate)
- ☐ Experience constant anxiety about never having enough money even when you do
- ☐ Believe that you must work hard or there needs to be a struggle in order to make money
- ☐ Think it is bad to be rich

Can you relate to this story or know someone who can?

I will always remember hearing a speaker point out that money is neutral. It's black and white, does not lie, and becomes whatever we think it is. Yet, think of the number of stories we hold around money—from "not being deserving or worthy" to "bad things happen if you make a lot of money." Consider the charges money (and money stories) cause in marriages and partnerships. Explosive fights. Divorce. Business partnerships dissolve. And if you analyze all those conflicts and experiences, I guarantee you will find layers of money-legacy stories and money story wounds. We also talk more about this in the chapter on stories and relationships.

Our stories around money are some of the most ingrained stories that keep us bound. Clients will come into my office to express their discontent around their jobs, relationships, or where they live and ask me to help them fix it. They will express their need to make a change because they are not happy, and experiencing health problems. When we get to the action steps to take toward their dreams, they find they are stuck and can't move, which is often due to a story about money. "I will not make as much money at a new job." "I can't afford to live on my own."

Though there may be truth in some of these stories, we need to talk about them and shed light on them so the story is not running your life or ruining your joy. Furthermore, our stories about money can block money from flowing into our lives. Who wants that? Not me. Not you. Yet, these stories are consuming most of our lives. Please trust me when I say to you, with gentle compassion: "you have a story about money." It is not a case where some people have them, and some do not. Every single person carries a story around money.

Most of us have money stories from our family of origin, which came from our parents' family of origin, and so on. If we do not illuminate these stories, they are just going to carry on and on a family money-legacy stories include:

- You have to work really hard to survive.
- If people give you money, you are a burden and made to feel guilty or shameful.
- To be considered successful, you have to have a lot of money.
- If I don't work 24/7, around the clock, I'll be homeless.
- Being rich is immoral.
- Being poor is terrible.

Research states that our stories about money are formed around age 10. We have all created a mindset toward money based on what our family believed or any experiences that we heard, saw, and witnessed around money. We take our money stories with us in everything we do. Money is tied up with and associated with feelings of worth, trust, addiction, and intellect.

We often see our money stories come to the surface in relationships. I remember grocery shopping with a college roommate, and as I watched her put everything in her cart, I felt like I would have a panic attack. Though I was unaware of the story underneath that emotional reaction at the time, now I can look back and connect to the messages I received in my upbringing. When I was growing up, you only bought what you needed because of our financial struggles. And I'm sure that story went back to my grandmother, who grew up during the Depression. So, while I watched my roommate stack our cart beyond what we needed, it went against a message I had stored in my DNA.

My roommate and I talked openly about the experience. Interestingly, she shared that they did not have much food growing up. As a result, she ensures that there is plenty now. Those are two different responses to similar money experiences, demonstrating how people can interpret a similar life experience differently.

Some people have had money their entire lives. They have never had to worry; they have more than enough and still carry money stories of lack, scarcity, and fear. In other words, despite their family not facing financial strife, messaging around money was ingrained and dictated their responses even when they had wealth.

Now, combine people sharing a home and finances who have differing money stories and contrasting reactions to those stories. What do you think happens? Most couples struggle with having even the most minor conversation around finances. It is no wonder it is one of the top reasons for divorce. Later in my chapter on Stories and Relationships, I expound on this subject and share tips on navigating money stories (and conflict) in your partnerships.

Let's face it, if you're living in the modern world, you're living in a capitalist society. Money runs this world. It determines many things from education, health care to what kind of car you drive and what house you live in and what clothes you wear. There is a serious charge around money. And there is so much shame and judgment around money, too. Talk about amplifying the charge!

In the podcast episode entitled *Money, Money, Money—Ain't it Funny?*, our brave participant helped us crack open some of our own potential stories around money by sharing how unique money stories were birthed in her past. In her case, a significant story was about the need to work really hard. The stories also touched upon making sure you do not get tricked. You can imagine what type of fight or flight survival state this participant could be in.

She also carried a story that being financially successful in business is somehow "dirty"—that it is better to help others and struggle because, "If you are experiencing abundance, then you must be taking advantage of someone." The participant admits that intellectually, she knows there are many win-win scenarios. Still, there are Parts of her that believe being wealthy is to be "sneaky," "bad," or "out-of-touch" because of some of the ways in which her family of origin and extended family history dictates how they earned their money or what happened to them when they had money.

One of the stories is about her paternal great-grandfather, who had found quite a bit of oil on the West Coast but was swindled out of all his shares and wealth by his business partner. She also shares how she witnessed her father go after money in an inauthentic way, leading her to believe she can't just go after money, because it feels inauthentic or immoral.

Another story derived from her past was the notion that "You have a taste of money, but then it goes away. "You can see it. You can taste it. But not have it." This story partly came from her father's being from a poor family, but a stepfather sent him to a private school, where he witnessed the very wealthy.

Transforming her stories would mean figuring out how to balance being a female entrepreneur aligned with her true desires and making a good profit. It is fascinating to consider all the layers of her ancestral stories around money. I feel fortunate to have her honesty and recounting of her family history recorded on this podcast as an inspiration for us all.

♫ The two songs that Mick and Tess Pulver prescribed for this participant to transform her money stories were: "From the Ashes" by Martina McBrinde and "Have a Little Faith in Me" by Jewel.

Stories around money are something I believe we all need to work on. I encourage you to take the time to go through your family tree and write down any possible stories that were passed down around money. Remember, this is not to shame or to judge. This is done with gentle curiosity and compassion in order to discover any family legacy stories that might be binding you and/or blocking the flow of money coming your way. One more thing—it is normal to have layers of money stories.

Journal Prompt: Make a family tree at least one or two generations back. Write a story around money for each ancestor based on what you know about them.

STORY #6

My chest is tightening; I must be having a heart attack.

"One of the number one reasons that people seek out my support is that they are uncomfortable with the physical sensations from anxiety or fear."
~ Jennifer H. Carey

Here's a quick checklist with some of the ways this story can come up in your life:

You or someone you know may:

- ☐ Constantly play out "what if" scenarios
- ☐ Make frequent doctors' appointments to check various ailments
- ☐ Carry a fear of having an anxiety or panic attack which keeps from leaving home or going to social gatherings
- ☐ Keep your social circle very small
- ☐ Be frozen and not step out of a comfort zone in any way, shape or form
- ☐ Have a persistent and constant worry about health that holds you back from the things you love to do

Can you relate to this story or know someone who can?

This section is one of the hardest for me to write for two reasons. One reason is that I fear it will come off as judgmental. So, let me give this disclaimer: I realize there are lots of complex reasons why people suffer from debilitating anxieties, from Obsessive Compulsive Disorder (ritualistic behaviors and rumination) to Agoraphobia (fear of leaving the house, being in crowded places, etc.). There are complex reasons for debilitating physical ailments, and physical pain and discomfort are valid. I experienced autoimmune and chronic pain flares, I understand. I hold all mental and physical ailments with deep compassion and grace. In this section, I intend to ensure that whatever story is associated with the psychological or physical challenge that is holding you back from living a life with joy and expression is illuminated. If you or a loved one suffers from stories similar to the one in this section, know that you or they are not alone. I am trying to meet you or them where you or they are and show you a possible trailhead that can bring you to healing that will help you live in less fear.

The second reason this is difficult is this story hits home. Beyond the many clients that I have had who have this debilitating story, there are two people near and dear to my heart who also suffer from this. They don't work. They don't go out with friends. They barely leave their home. The only step they take outside of their comfort zone is to go to appointments with various doctors who are all searching for a physical or medical diagnosis of something that, in my opinion, is more psychosocial, mental, and behavioral than physical. In my humble yet professional opinion, what starts as a physical sensation and ailment gets translated into the worst-case scenario and becomes mental. The physical manifestation becomes an easy excuse to avoid the world. These two things feed on each other. As a result, what may be something that the body can heal and recover from through a combination of Western Medicine and holistic healing turns into anxiety, and all the stories and beliefs they carry that keep them locked up. Fear of social situations. The fear and stress of making a mistake at a job or school. The fear of germs. The fear of _____ (fill in the blank). Anxiety of any form. It gets to a point where it is hard to know which comes first. Making all of this worse is denial and a complete lack of awareness that all of these things are getting in the way of living a fully expressed and joyful life.

Again, this is not to discount their physical ailments or challenges. I validate them and understand chronic pain. As I mentioned before, I have suffered from chronic pain. I know some readers may not agree with what I am about to say, but here it goes: staying home consistently does NOT make you better. It does not heal you. We need fresh air. We need interactions and connections with other people. We need challenges, growth, and stimulation. Avoidance is not the antidote. Avoidance feeds the isolation that makes us feel alone and sick. For some reason, our society still holds a stigma around mental health. It's so much better than generations before, yet still today, there is more comfort focusing on the physical focus rather than the mental.

Let us inspire and illuminate the stories of people staying in their homes, not contributing to society (a healthy need), and not taking risks (a healthy need) for fear that they may feel stressed, have a panic attack, or experience physical pain. Getting out could help heal their physical ailments or, at the very least, help make them more manageable. Let us uncover the blind spot that may be covering the path to healing for individuals suffering in this way. There is a possibility that anyone believing that it is unsafe to go outside may not be aware that it is a story, narrative, or belief that is keeping them from experiencing the things of pure joy in this life that all exist outside of their door. If you can relate to this experience and stories around it and are happy, healthy, and content living an insular and isolated life, then this section may not be for you. On the other hand, if you are someone (or know someone) who knows there is more to life than the confines of your home, read on.

When our brave participant of the podcast episode entitled *Heart Attack or Panic Attack* reached out to share her story of not leaving her home for fear that she was having a heart attack when it was a panic attack, it was like a massive gust of fresh air filled my office. I exclaimed: "YES! Someone young is speaking out about this. Let's do this and break the bonds of so many out there!" She was beyond courageous when she chose not to be anonymous. She felt strongly about letting people know who she is to be able to relate to and heal from this even more. What is so powerful about her message is that you can access empathy and compassion for people who fear something is wrong with their health. You also learn that asking and receiving mental health is a great step in turning things around. That is what changed and continues to change things for her.

Health Anxiety, formerly referred to as Hypochondria, started for this participant, named Savannah, when her parents decided to sell her childhood home that her parents built with their own hands and move to Florida at the same time Savannah was moving to Florida to start college. Health Anxiety began the day they moved. The physical changes triggered physical ailments. At the time, she was 18 years old and did not know what anxiety was. Furthermore, Savannah had no idea that physical ailments, like chest tightening or headaches, could be related to mental and emotional conditions. She had no name for what was happening and just thought it was a heart attack. Then, the story began, "When my chest tightens, it means I am having a heart attack." Savannah admits that a story is still there but not as strongly, and she is working on it, evident in her self-awareness and insight. Savannah's healing journey around this is also obvious in her interactions, courage to step outside of her comfort zone, and how she continues to transform this story.

This story led Savannah to slowly not be able to function normally. She did not want to leave the house, then her bedroom, and then she didn't even want to leave her bed. Then the ruminating thoughts came: "When am I going to die? How am I going to die?" Savannah would obsessively take her pulse and avoided sleeping on her left side for fear that it would contribute to what she thought was a heart condition. When her parents sent her to the doctors, tests found no problems. She was then referred to a therapist who helped her translate the anxiety into creative expression. And that was the moment things changed and started to turn for the better for Savannah. She asked for help even with the fear that people would not understand what was happening to her or dismiss it.

Everything shifted when, one day, she learned there was a name for what she was experiencing: Anxiety. It was enlightening when she realized that what she was experiencing was beyond physical health. Suddenly, she learned that there was a name for it and symptoms backed by scientific reasons that explained why it was happening. With this newfound awareness, little by little, Savannah felt more and more empowered to face the anxiety and learn from it instead of being paralyzed by it.

In the episode, Savannah shared that mindfulness was the most helpful tool in turning the corner in her healing journey. Mindfulness or present moment awareness helped her break down and understand the pattern she was experiencing into small parts. First, Savannah would feel anxiety or nervousness; then, there would be a tightness in her chest. When the tightness in her chest happened, she started to think she was having a heart attack. That would take her to the worst-case scenario: death. Once that worst-case scenario entered her mind, she would feel constantly in fear and on edge that the pattern would start from the first step and repeat. Avoidance of anything anxiety-inducing felt like the best way to stay alive.

Savannah spoke to the art of learning how to respond to emotions and sensations rather than reacting. In other words, now, when she experiences that first symptom of nervousness, she is able to sit with the discomfort and name it for what it is: anxiety. She allows it to pass rather than going into a downward spiral about being in poor physical health and calling off plans to connect, socialize, and get out in the world. Savannah now decides to respond rather than react. She feels the discomfort, naming it, taming it, and letting it pass by. One thing is for sure: our feelings pass if we let them. We have the choice not only to respond versus react but also to choose not to attach to them. All of this falls under mindfulness practices, and these are the tools Savannah now swears by to help her with her health anxiety.

People land on my couch in my office because their emotions of sadness, anger, and fear are uncomfortable. They want the feeling to disappear. They beg me to help make the feeling disappear. They may use drugs, alcohol, food, sex, or even prescription medication to numb the feelings and make it go away. The two people near and dear to me that I mentioned earlier had a numbing agent or reaction to the discomfort—it was avoidance. If you do not leave the house, put yourself in uncomfortable social situations, work, etc, you do not have to feel anxiety or discomfort.

My goal is to help my clients learn and understand emotions and empower them to befriend them. Whether I use Parts Work or another form of therapy, I try to help them meet the physical or emotional sensations that are uncomfortable with compassion and curiosity. Rather than feeling the need to push away, avoid, or numb, we should treat our emotions or physical ailments like a signal from mind, body, and soul—that there is a message to be heard and they have the power to respond rather than react.

Savannah, I salute you. You are doing this, and you are doing it at such a young age. Thank you for coming on this podcast to inspire others that there is a different way of responding and that we can choose a different story to associate with the discomfort of anxiety. Your health anxiety and stories around it no longer lead your life. I cannot wait to see you continue to shift this story and feel free, playful, and curious without the "what ifs" paralyzing you.

🎵 Singer-songwriter Shannon Ward and I prescribed two songs for the participant: "I Hope You Dance" by Lee Ann Womack, with the lyrics: "When you get the choice to sit it out or dance, I hope you dance," and "Freedom" by George Michael because freedom is what she feels when this story no longer leads her.

> **Journal Prompt:** Explore any physical sensations that cause discomfort and worry. Engage in a dialogue with these sensations, asking them what they're trying to communicate. Approach this exercise with gentle curiosity and compassion, allowing the answers and messages from your body to flow naturally.

Story #7

I'm Not Enough Nor Worthy to Live My Dreams
(I'm Not Enough and/or I'm Too Much stories)

"You are worthy of your dreams."
~ Jennifer H. Carey

Here's a quick checklist with some of the ways this story can come up in your life:

You or someone you know may:

- ☐ Experience a persistent worry after a social situation that you were too much
- ☐ Not believe there is enough time nor money for you to achieve your dreams
- ☐ Put others first: take care of others because following your dreams is selfish
- ☐ Carry a disbelief that you possess the talent or ability to live your dreams
- ☐ Experience a sense of stuckness, loss or confusion

Can you relate to this story or know someone who can?

The stories around "not being enough" or "I am too much" are all too common, and they get you "coming and going." Let me explain by describing one of my patterns. First, I get the sense that someone I know needs something. They may need advice, a good meal, or my healing time and presence. I give them one or more of these things. Suddenly, something shifts, and it feels like they are pulling away after I have done the act of kindness I felt moved to perform. Then, the stories begin. I'll start to play the story in my head that what I did was not enough, which is why they pulled away. So, I give some more and maybe even reach out to ensure everything is okay. Now, the story playing in my head is I am too much. See? These stories get you coming and going.

You often see or hear about this story with people just starting to date. They worry they are not good enough for the person. At the same time, they worry that if they are too expressive, show too much of themselves, or are too open (not playing hard to get), then they are too much and will push the person away. See? Coming and going.

There are so many ways that these two stories come up in people's lives, preventing them from the vulnerability that is needed to express themselves fully and follow their dreams. Because these stories get you coming and going, there can be a sense of stuckness, loss, or confusion. The podcast episode, *I'm Not Enough Nor Worthy of My Dreams* is rich with lessons around these stories. The brave participant in this episode shares how he has been incorporating the story of I'm not good enough: Baseline. He shares that he is not good enough to live the life he wants, have the job, or have the relationship he deserves. He can't have the life he wants to live.

The participant elaborates on all of his stories about his self-worth. One of these stories is: "I'm not good enough to be an artist, so I will just do what I can get." He takes us back to the story he interpreted from his family of origin: "I have to take care of everything around me before I can take care of myself." "I have to serve my family before I serve myself." As we know, our family of origin is where our stories come from. They mean well. The roles and dynamics are born from a system. When we are young and our brain is still developing, we absorb messages and experiences from our family system like a sponge. It is hard not to continue living the script written for us during our early development.

Before recording this podcast, this participant was engaged to be married and had ambitious plans to have a family but then ended up calling off the engagement. Is this him playing out the story that he does not deserve to follow his dreams, or did he try not to live under the stories and expectations his family set upon him? Only he can answer that. His dreams. His heart. Whatever the actual reason he called off the engagement, this work intends to ensure that it is not a false belief or story that gets in the way of him realizing anything he wants in this life.

With gentle curiosity, please take note if you find yourself telling yourself that, "You are not enough" or, "You are too much." Take notice, whether at work or in relationships with family or friends. I know this may be a far leap, but I am telling you again: you are whole. You are perfectly imperfect. You are complete. You are a star. You were born to shine and destined to live out your dreams. Please do not let either of these stories leave you feeling stuck.

🎵 The song prescribed to the participant by Mick and Tess Pulver was

"Hoochie Coochie Man" by Muddie Waters. The lyrics and energy of this song are all about claiming who you are.

Journal Prompt: Describe a time where fears around being "too much" or "not enough" got in the way of you stepping toward your dreams.

Taking a Closer Look at Dichotomies and Holding Opposing Thoughts

In the above episode, we delve into a concept likely to resonate with many: the dichotomy of "I'm not enough" and "I'm too much." These extreme self-perceptions can often lead to tension and distress in our relationships as we view life in black and white rather than the nuanced gray it truly is.

This phenomenon of black-and-white thinking comes up a lot in my work with individuals and couples. This rigid thinking makes individuals and couples feel trapped or stuck in one way of being. The antidote is to zoom out, soften our gaze, and see the gray and what lies in between our extreme thinking. In the chapter on stories and relationships, I expound on this tool to see the layers of stories rather than locking ourselves and each other into one extreme belief. It is one hundred percent possible for two opposing thoughts to be held simultaneously in a way that assists us in our relationships with ourselves and others and decreases the tension.

When we shift our perspective from black and white to gray, tension lessens within ourselves and with each other. Let's use the two stories from the above podcast episode. If we illuminate those two stories and work to neutralize them to shift our perspective, this is an example of what can happen:

I'm not enough.

Close up, the story "I'm not enough" is paralyzing because, with this story, you do not believe in yourself or your capability to do or be anything. When you zoom out and take a step back, soften your gaze, and look at "I'm not enough" with gray lenses (versus black and white), you can begin to test its validity. Who, what, and how is that a standard for human existence and journey? How on earth is there a definition of "enough" related to humans? It's helpful and healthy when we judge food as cooked enough, and it's damaging when we look at ourselves and other humans as enough or not. For example, is there enough water to boil the pasta? Is there enough beauty in that human to be loved? Who on earth defines such a thing in the latter question? Aren't we all perfectly imperfect? Let's eliminate the category of enoughness as a description of ourselves and others and see us all as unique, whole, perfect, and complete. Nobody else can be you.

I'm too much.

Close up, with the story: "I'm too much", your fully expressed life is blocked by hiding your light because you are afraid to shine—another lose-lose situation. We are left with a similar question when we step away from the black-and-white interpretation of this story and give a softening of perspective. Who defines what "too much" is? And how do we put people in that category? Perhaps someone is "too much" for another person, but that defines the other person and what they can tolerate; it doesn't define the person that is "too much."

The next time you feel distressed with yourself or a partner, check in and see if you're thinking in extremes or black and white. A simple warning sign is when you are labeling something in extremes such as always and never. Describing something as always or never signals that you have entered a place of extreme judgment and are in a zone of opinion, rather than fact. Humans are too complex to be categorized into extreme boxes. Allow yourself and others to be more sophisticated than a simple label. We have too many labels, from social and economic class, ethnic and cultural background, belief systems, and political views. As a collective, we love categories and boxes. Sometimes, they can be helpful. Things we need to control for our health can benefit from black-and-white thinking. For example, addiction of any kind benefits from thinking in absolutes (e.g., not drinking alcohol, not eating sugar or cholesterol, not smoking or doing drugs). It is when these thoughts are destructive that we need to try and shift our perspective. When it comes to being in your healthiest and best form, you may need to think in extremes. However, there are far more examples of things in this life being in the gray.

By zooming out and shifting perspective from black and white to gray, we can soften the harshness and damage of specific stories we hold. Softening in this way adds compassion, non judgment, and an openness that allows for something new and unlimited to be born. Yes, we humans are simple in the sense that we all need to survive and crave love and be loved. That part of us is simple, but the rest is more complex.

Journal Prompt: Write about when you held a story of being "too much" or "not enough." Then step back, soften, and see it through gray lenses. Write about seeing it with more layers and less extreme views.

CHAPTER 2

✳

Parts Work *and* Illuminating the Stories that Bind Us

I know I already mentioned Internal Family Systems (IFS), and I will continue to do so. To say that I love this approach is an understatement. It makes complete sense to me, and it is a language that I use to help heal myself and my clients. I also use it to understand my loved ones and my relationships with them. It complements the journey of awareness of the stories that are holding us back in so many ways.

Defining Self in IFS

Richard Swartz created this phenomenal therapeutic approach, and much of this foundation comes from his wisdom. In this approach, we arrive into this life with our Self: a leader within, with all of the "C qualities" I list below. It is at our core. Every one of us has access to these qualities if we so choose. Our Self, in IFS, becomes the conduit to help us self-connect, self-understand and self-heal. It holds the following characteristics, which are called the 8 Cs and 5 Ps.

The goal of Internal Family Systems is to build our Self (with a capital S).

The 8 C's are:
- Calm
- Clarity
- Courage
- Connectedness
- Confidence
- Creativity
- Curiosity
- Compassion

The 5 P's are:
- Playfulness
- Patience
- Presence
- Perspective
- Persistence

Parts in IFS

Again, we are born with those Self qualities. Then, as life moves along, we hit some bumps of trauma and family dynamics within our family of origin, and various Parts of us are born to manage, protect, and navigate those bumps. Some common Parts are The People Pleaser, The Inner Critic, and The Perfectionist. You can find definitions of these parts in the back of the book. Dr. Richard Schwartz teaches us to become more self-aware by getting to know these Parts deeper in the same way this book encourages you to investigate our stories. Also, similar to our stories, we need to get to know the Parts by approaching them with a neutral, calm, curious, and compassionate energy.

One of the most reassuring aspects of IFS is its non-judgmental approach towards our stories and Parts. It emphasizes that they are merely Parts of us, not our entire identity. Our Parts, like the stories we carry, do not define us. None of these Parts are viewed as 'bad 'in this approach. Richard Schwartz's book, *No Bad Parts*, underscores this perspective. Most of these Parts have a purpose or intention to protect, manage, or help. Even our destructive Parts, such as addiction Parts, are trying to assist us by numbing intense discomfort. These Parts can be assets when in balance. The issues or conflicts within our systems arise when the Parts become extreme or lose trust in Self. In *No Bad Parts*, Dr. Schwartz points out that, "many of our troubles come not so much from the Part itself, but from our panic about it, because we believe it defines us and won't end."

The empowering journey is rebuilding our system so that there is trust in the Self to lead our internal system and, again, this acknowledgment that the story the Part is saying does not define us and is not the be all and end all. Similar to our human needs, when we work with different Parts of ourselves, they want to be acknowledged, heard, understood and loved. Parts work is giving our Parts this opportunity. My favorite analogy is thinking of Self as a conductor of an orchestra. And all of the musicians are the Parts. You may call up various Parts at certain times. You may even have two musicians perform a duet. However, sometimes you do not want the Part or instrument to play. You certainly do not want one instrument to overpower all other instruments. You want harmony, with Self in the lead. Self is the conductor of these Parts instead of them being in control of us.

Parts Work and Illuminating Our Stories

By combining IFS and *Illuminating the Stories that Bind Us*, we can identify the Parts of ourselves that are telling the story that are holding us back. Take my story of needing to make everything okay for everyone. That is my People Pleaser Part. People Pleaser, when out of balance, can work to an extreme to ensure I am loved and accepted. When in balance and Self is in the lead, People Pleaser is a considerate and thoughtful asset in my system. When People Pleaser carries a false belief or story that I need to do everything for everyone to be loved, we have a problem in our system. By getting to know my People Pleaser, I can further understand where that Part comes from and why it holds that false belief.

The illumination of that process allows for clarity and connection to that distinct Part in a profound and meaningful way. You learn not only the intention of the Part and the story it carries but also what that Part needs to feel calm and able to step back into your internal system. That process alone is putting the Self in the lead. When Self is in the lead, everything shifts so that the Part and the stories are no longer in control, hijacking our lives and reactions and taking over and running the show. When our Parts are in control, the stories are in control. When the Self is leading, we can self-heal and self-clarify our stories. As a result, we can come from a clear, confident, and calm place rather than a wounded and most likely distorted story.

An essential aspect of this work is that when Self is in the lead , and our Parts are balanced, we can utilize our various Parts as assets and consultants. People volunteer to do my podcast because they are experiencing a strong physical or emotional pattern that is disturbing their peace and holding them back. Using the stories we illuminated in this chapter and connecting them with Parts formally taught in IFS, we can enhance the process of illumination, restoring the Parts to a more balanced and constructive stage.

Before we connect the stories from this chapter with the names of Parts, remember that we need to approach these Parts the same way we need to identify our stories: with curiosity and compassion versus judgment. If any of these parts resonate with you, there is a key in the back that you can refer to to understand the part further.

Story: *I'm not enough for my family.*
Parts: The People Pleaser, The Inner Critic, The Caretaker, The Perfectionist, The Conformist, The Guilt Tripper

Story: *I am bad and deserve to be punished.*
Parts: The Saboteur, The Procrastinator, The Destroyer, The Defensive Part

Story: *The reason he doesn't love me anymore is because I'm not _____ (pretty, intelligent, rich…) enough.*
Parts: The Guarded/Defender, The Codependent, The Over Thinker

Story: *I am an imposter.*
Parts: The Imposter, The Social Anxiety, The Paranoid, The Perfectionist, The Underminer

Story: *It is better to help others and struggle, because if you are experiencing abundance, you must be taking advantage of someone.*
Parts: The Inferior, The Financially Anxious, The Workaholic, The Skeptic

Story: *My chest is tightening—I must be having a heart attack.*
Parts: The Health Anxiety, The Saboteur, The Social Anxiety, The Paranoid

Story: *I'm not enough, nor worthy to live my dreams. ("I'm not enough" and/or "I'm too much" stories)*
Parts: The Inferior, The Inner critic, The People Pleaser, The Perfectionist

The specific names of Parts that I used here are names that are officially recognized in IFS. One of my favorite things about naming our Parts is we can activate our healing imagination by creating unique names for our Parts. For example, I have a Scheduler part. This Part ensures I make appointments, get through my to-do list, etc. He balances out my Daisy Field Part, who has no sense of time and wants to be in the daisy field, reciting poems and exploring the wonder of nature.

Journal Prompt: Which Part from the stories above frequently hijacks your system? With curiosity and compassion, ask the Part two questions:
1. What is its intention and purpose in taking over your system? Listen and write what comes up.
2. What practice or quality does this Part need to calm down in your system? Listen and write what comes up.

CHAPTER 3

⁕

The Foundation Before Moving Forward

In any form of therapy or personal growth, it is essential to set the foundation of psychological safety for healing growth to prosper. Vulnerability needs a safe space to sprout. In individual therapy, where it is just the therapist and client, this foundation may be more implicit and something I or any other therapist creates through rapport-building skills like empathy. In larger groups, explicitly teaching these agreements and guidelines is essential. With groups, you have more personalities and more people contributing to the healing, learning, and growing space, and you need everyone to be on the same page in building that sense of safety and support.

Many of our stories have been shoved deep down and hidden within ourselves. When we bring them to light, it may be the first time we expose them. Therefore, our Parts and their stories must feel seen, heard, valued, and understood. Don't believe me? The next time you feel like someone is not listening to you or appreciating what you are saying, watch your Defensive Part shoot up so fast and escalate and distract from the flow of the conversation.

When we hold the posture of non-judgment, we (and our Parts) feel safe to share our stories. Here are the necessary bricks in that foundation that will help as you take this illuminating journey with me:

1. **Non-Judgement:** To heal, learn, and grow, we need space from our Inner Critic, Skeptic, or Judge. Trust whatever comes up for you in this process; you do not need to judge it as right or wrong, good or bad. Trust your intuition and innate ability to heal. The energy will go where it needs to. Often, when we bring something to light, we can have a knee-jerk reaction of judgment and criticism. These Parts show up to make sure your system stays safe. However, they may not be as helpful as they think they are. Notice if Critic, Skeptic, or Judge enter the stage by criticizing or judging, and gently request that they stay on the side stage while you sort this out. They can witness the process but not interfere. When you notice them and respectfully ask them to step aside so that you can build a healthy relationship with your Part/story, your Part will feel more comfortable to elaborate and help you learn more about it. Note: These Parts often appear when you are also working on something creative.

2. **Gentle Curiosity:** I love the term gentle curiosity. It feels like an innocent child, full of wonder, learning and exploring something with neutrality and investigation. As you begin illuminating the stories binding you, please be gentle and curious with yourself and your stories. Gathering information is an integral part of any process. When we are gently curious about getting to know our Parts and stories, we gather rich information that helps us understand ourselves. Knowledge is power, and it starts with an openness and willingness to learn.

3. **Compassion:** Again, when we bring our stories to light, either by writing them down or saying them aloud, there can be a lot of judgment and shame. After all, they have stayed hidden in our subconscious for a reason. Please shine a compassionate light on all of it. Every single aspect of this process shines a light of compassion. Remember, in the section on IFS, these stories and Parts are often born out of traumatic experiences or, at the very least, challenging dynamics, such as your family of origin. These stories think they are serving you and doing you good. If you are struggling to give your Parts and stories compassion, think about how you would treat an innocent child going through what you are going through or how you would treat your best friend. See if that helps you flex your compassionate muscles.

4. **Persistence:** In my own experience and the experiences of my clients

and participants on my podcast, persistence is critical because our stories do not entirely disappear overnight. Indeed, they will begin to dissolve and lose their charge overnight, but there will still be layers to peel away. Again, please do not let that discourage you because every little bit helps. Don't lose hope! Keep going when you want to give up. Your emotions and reactions will be less and less charged and intense the more you shed light and illuminate the stories fueling them. Just keep on your path of healing and take the action steps to interrupt and transform your binding stories so you can live up to your fullest expression and highest potential in this life.

WORKSHEET

Illuminating the Stories that Are Binding You

Start using this worksheet to shed light on the story that's holding you back. By giving it a name, you gain the power to control it. Remember to approach this process with curiosity and compassion. For best results, ask your Critic and Judge Parts to step aside while you work through this worksheet.

1. Identify a charged emotional pattern that you notice in your life, such as recurring anger, sadness, fear, fight, flight, or freeze. This could be a general response or a reaction to a specific situation. For instance, if you feel anxious and avoid dating despite wanting to meet someone, that's a charged emotional pattern forming an obstacle between you and what you want.

2. Make a list of all the thoughts (stories) you have associated with this emotional pattern (e.g., I'm not good enough for a relationship, I'm undeserving of a healthy partner).

3. Choose which thought is the most potent narrative/story running in your mind and disturbing your peace.

4. When do you think this story began? Describe.

5. How has this story limited you in your life or made you stuck? Explain.

6. What would your life be like without this story?

Bonus Question: Which Part of you is telling the story you wrote above (e.g., The People Pleaser? The Perfectionist? The Inner Critic? The Imposter?)

CHAPTER 4

※

Stories in Relationships

There is nothing like a heated discussion to trigger childhood wounds, especially with our romantic partners. I will never forget Marianne Williamson sharing in a talk about how arguments with our romantic partners often boil down to a conflict between two childhood wounds rather than between the actual adults themselves. She described how our perfectly matched partners hold up a mirror to our childhood wounds so that we can heal them. Bringing us back to IFS and Parts Work, often the Parts born in our childhood to manage and protect us have childlikeness to them even though we are adults. You better believe that with those wounds and with those Parts come our stories.

Often, when doing couples work and witnessing a couple trying to understand one another, in my imagination I start to see a curtain of unhealed stories between them. What do I mean by this? You can see how one partner shares something, and the other interprets it entirely differently. As I, the third party, observe, it is as if one partner says a statement that goes through this imaginary curtain of unhealed stories, and the partner listening hears something unrelated to what the partner speaking meant. This imaginary curtain has a filter that holds the listener's stories or wounds, and the speaker's statement is translated or interpreted through that lens. As the objective party, I can offer a different perspective and translation and help each partner uncover the stories between them, understanding each other more precisely and straightforwardly.

Do you think you have that imaginary unhealed story curtain that filters what someone else says to you through a false belief that you are holding? We 100% use our stories to interpret what someone else is saying. They say, "I cannot do that today; I'm too busy," and our curtain of unhealed stories tells us: "You do not care about me. I am not important." Now, that is just the story interpretation part. Then comes the *reaction* to that story. Mix that all up with some past trauma, and you now have a heated discussion or argument. Raise your hand if your partner says something, and you shut down, cry, and go from 0-100 on the anger scale. Did you raise your hand? If we could see this played out in front of us like a movie, we could see how someone we love and know loves us becomes an enemy out to get us, and the stories feed and reinforce that interpretation.

As a couples therapist, it's an absolute honor to say "time out" and help them with that imaginary curtain full of unhealed stories born of traumatic or difficult events in that person's life. From there, awareness and understanding can start to change the emotional and behavioral response patterns from the misinterpretation. The knowledge and techniques in this section help us save our friendships, collaborations with colleagues, marriages and romantic relationships, business partners, family connections, and beyond. This section will increase awareness and compassion around the situation, giving it much light and liberation. Research proves time and time again that the quality of our relationships is relative to our level of happiness. Let's learn ways to improve our relationships and make them healthier so we can all be happier. Let's go!

The *Layers of Stories* Technique: a Must-Have Relationship Tool

This technique aims to learn and take away the important lessons of a heated conflict and misunderstanding instead of staying stuck in a state of confusion, hurt, or resentment. It also aims to bring healing to some of the layers for each party that get in the way of healthy and fulfilling relationships.

Now, let's walk through the steps of the Layers of Stories Technique together. To make it more engaging, I'll share some personal examples. These will help you see how to apply this tool in your own life. I've also included a section of Frequently Asked Questions. Make sure to read it for extra tips on improving your relationships with this technique.

Premise: You have a heated disagreement or conflict with someone in your life, such as a partner, friend, colleague, etc., as evidenced by a fight-flight-freeze response, defensiveness, or emotional charge.

Step #1: Take a time-out. You do not want to continue this conversation or make any significant decisions when you are in a highly emotional state. Separate and go to a safe and calming place. Bring paper and a pen to write. Wait until you are calm and neutral, where you can be compassionate and curious with yourself. Do breathing exercises or walk in nature to help you find your inner calm.

Step #2: Each person in the conflict or disagreement writes down every story, fact, or opinion related to the charge and intensity of the disagreement. I often like to make two columns: one for stories I hold about myself and another person, and the other for what stories I THINK the other person has about me and the situation.

- Stories about yourself related to the disagreement, including any wounds you are aware of

- Stories you hold about the other person and any of their wounds you are aware of

- Stories you think the other person is holding about you

*Please refer to page 76-81 for a visual diagram labeled, *Worksheet for Layers of Stories Technique* that can help guide you through this process.

Step #3: Review each story and check in with yourself. Is the story coming from a place of Fear or Love? Write Fear or Love next to each story based on your assessment.

Step #4: (optional) If you are familiar with Internal Family Systems or Parts Work, revisit your list of stories in step 2 and name the Part you think that story comes from.

Step #5: Take a moment to consider other factors that may have contributed to the argument. Some examples can include:

- Defensiveness

- Blame

- Lack of sleep or lack of self-care

- Outside stressors that you and the other party may be dealing with

- Hunger

- Alcohol or substance influences

- Societal stories or norms

- Generational trauma

- Hormones

- Cultural differences

- Sub-cultural differences

- Prejudices based on socioeconomic status, ethnic backgrounds, political and religious viewpoints, sexual orientation and gender identity or age

- A childhood wound or traumatic event from the past that feels similar to this

Important Considerations for Step #5

Prejudices around ethnic background and socioeconomic status can bind us and impact our relationships and communication. Let's not forget how religious beliefs and political differences can do the same, as well as our prejudices of people based on their sexual orientation, gender identity, or even their age. The most powerful and influential thing we can do is be aware of our judgments and challenge them because we never know someone else's journey or story, so it is incredibly unfair to project our preconceived notions onto them. Taking time to bring our judgments and stories front and center is an incredible gift we give ourselves, our family, our friends, and our society.

It is essential and empowering that we take the time to be more aware of factors in this step. With gentle curiosity, non-judgment, and compassion, I encourage you to consider these factors in this step. This step may be challenging, yet it is vital. Looking at our prejudices and biases can be tricky because, often, we aren't even aware we have them. When you uncover a prejudgement or extreme viewpoint, please do not let Shame Parts hijack the process. We all prejudge. Your showing up for yourself and the other person in this way is an incredible gift. Honesty with yourself and the other person about how an extreme belief or story may impact the conflict will only bring you more clarity, peace, and resolution.

I wish we were required to take multicultural and diversity classes in high school to illuminate some of the stories about others ingrained in our cells at an early age. We would ALL be better humans. We would become aware of the detrimental stories we project onto people because of race or status that aren't even accurate. It's incredibly enlightening. I remember when I had to do it in my Multicultural Counseling course in graduate school. It was incredibly enlightening. At the end of the course, I wanted to run to a mountaintop and scream all that I had learned and realized. The journey is ongoing, but it allows us to bring judgments and stories that we hold front and center so they do not destroy our relationships with others and ourselves. In future sections relating to the stories other people place on us and gossip, I explore further how judgment, shame, and prejudices can impact the health of our relationships.

Step #6: Set aside a safe and neutral time for each of you to come together and share your stories. Take turns by giving each person 10-15 minutes; during that time, one person speaks, and the other listens. There is no defensiveness or apologies. If a Defensive Part arises, gently notice it and ask it to step aside. Breathe and resume listening. And if an Overapologetic Part comes up, the same thing applies - gentle acknowledgment and asking it to step aside unless called upon. You each get to experience your stories heard, seen, and healed. After all, remember that they're just stories. Yes, maybe there is some truth in them; however, most of them come from hurt, childhood wounds, trauma, etc. Our goal is not who is right or wrong here. Our goal is to illuminate the stories that are binding the relationship so that you can break free of the stories together. You can choose a healthier and more constructive story for your relationship.

Important Considerations for Step #6
I write about compassion and curiosity for yourself and your stories many times in this book. During this step, it is vital to also practice curiosity and compassion for the other person. Treat them and their stories how you would want yourself and your stories to be treated. Remember that most of the emotional charge stems from a childhood wound or traumatic experience before you came into the picture.

If you try this step and share your stories with the other person, and it quickly escalates to pain, defensiveness, and inability to hear the other person, then you likely need to press pause again and wait for a better time. You may also need to choose a place like a café or a place in nature to have some other soothing factors to help ground you. Another option is to do this exercise with a therapist or a mediator.

I know there are sayings that people advise us about: "Don't go to bed angry" or "Don't let the sun go down on your anger," but sometimes we need to agree to disagree until we can discuss it more constructively. It's okay to wait. We are usually better and clearer in the morning anyway. You can say: "I love you, and we'll discuss this later."

In conclusion, the Layers of Stories Technique brings much richness and depth to healing the relationship with yourself and others. I have included three real-life examples below. One scenario happened with a mother figure—the other with my husband, and the third with a friend. In the first two of these situations, I met with the other person and applied Step #5 of this technique. Step #5, or coming together to share our stories, has not happened for the third scenario. However, you will see that I still gleaned a lot of growth and healing by applying the Layers of Stories Technique by myself. As I mentioned, I encourage you to practice this tool whether or not the other person is willing to do so. Sometimes, we can only control ourselves. Utilize that power.

REAL-LIFE STORY AND APPLICATION #1

When Someone's Protection Spurs Hurt

Thinking back to where our stories come from and our section on Parts Work at the beginning of this book, remember how important context is in understanding what is beneath our behaviors. Our stories come from patterns within our context, whether it's family, society, culture, friends, etc. The system in which our stories are born is important.

This system/context example comes from my relationship with the mother of my high school sweetheart. Let's call her Joan. Joan and I have remained extremely close, and she became a mother figure during my formative years. We have remained so close that after she sold her home of over 25 years, she moved to live near me for a few years. The original story/disagreement I am about to share took place years before I developed this technique. It was when she moved closer to me, and we were able to come together to heal and make sense of what happened in our disagreement, that this technique was born.

Here's the context: Joan and her daughter and grandchildren visited me for a few nights. My husband and I were only dating at the time and living separately. At that time, I was completing my supervision hours for licensure as a mental health counselor. The critical detail around that fact is that when you are getting your supervision hours, it is like a paid internship. Therefore, my salary was half what it was in my previous job, and I was struggling to live on my own financially. It was the end of a long summer day in the sun—note that factor of the story. Joan, her daughter, and her grandchildren had just traveled on a family trip in upstate New York, so everyone was tired—note that layer of the story. Joan was drinking gin and tonic. Alcohol should always be pointed out as a factor in this technique because alcohol skews judgment, tone, body language, and other aspects of effective communication. We ended up having a very emotional interaction. She confronted me on the fact that my then-boyfriend, now husband, was not helping me financially. She expressed concern and judgment about ways that he could be helping me. I was defensive, offended, and emotional. I remember going into the bathroom with her daughter, also a dear friend, and sobbing. Everyone was upset after this conversation. Why? There must be layers of stories to identify.

Nine years later, Joan and I are discussing this event as an attempt to heal and make sense of it. We both remembered its intensity. How do we heal this?

We started to go through the layers of stories, facts and factors that each of us held around that interaction.

My Side:

- My boyfriend at that time, who is now my husband, was going through a difficult divorce, and he was only separated. Therefore, supporting me in any way would make things more complicated. He was still in a 50/50 marriage.

- Until then, my adult life had been independent, and I was only used to supporting myself. I was not used to receiving financial support, so that was not natural for me at that moment.

- Joan is the mother of my young love. She was a mother figure during my formative years; her opinion on anything in my life means a lot to me and holds weight.

- Enter the "what if" monsters: What if she was right? What if this person could be supporting me and he is not? What does that say about him? What does that say about me and my worth?

Note: When you have an intense and surprising emotional reaction, it often involves worth or loss. In this case, I was feeling my story and fear around self-worth, which intensified the tears. Worth and shame can cause a ton of charge, make things come out sideways, and spiral into heated conversations if those stories are hidden, unhealed, and we are unaware. Our stories and interpretations around worth and loss are the most vulnerable.

Joan's Side:

- She grew up in a time when men supported women. That was the norm. A woman was married by the time she was 20 years old, and she cared for the home and family and was supported by her husband.

- After Joan got divorced, she became incredibly independent and financially successful without the help of a man. She often was the breadwinner in relationships, but she did not want this for me, her adopted daughter.

- As a mother figure, she wanted to ensure that I was and would be cared for financially and otherwise.

Reading those facts and factors, listed and broken down, can you see how the emotional intensity starts to lose its charge? You start to see and understand both sides. Bringing both sides to light in this way, they can be held simultaneously in a cocoon of rich and complicated layers. Remember the section in Chapter 1 on dichotomies and holding both? Life and relationships are too complex to try and shove everything in a box of extreme black-and-white judgments. When we illuminate the stories that bind us in this way, awareness and clarity of the layers suddenly allow us to be more creative and compassionate in navigating the conflict. When you work through this technique independently, you gain more self-awareness and an understanding of your side of the street, which alone can be fruitful. When you have the privilege of having the other person a part of the process, think of how healing and growth-inspiring that can be for your relationship with them and yourself.

Some of you may be wondering: what if she was right? What if this "intervention" of sorts from Joan was something that needed to be said, and you needed to run for the hills from your then-boyfriend? Step #3, regarding discernment of love vs. fear, is helpful for these questions or concerns. As we know, much worry and concern can be around money. Taking the time to discern whether the story is coming from a place of fear and love is valuable.

There is also the possibility that both of us could be right. There could be elements of what Joan said that had truth and elements on my side that are true. Both can simultaneously be true. Again, this is the gray stuff in many arguments that I witness as a couple's counselor, and it is possible to find elements of truth within both sides and in their stories. Knowing that alone can take away the charge in your conflicts moving forward. It drops the tension often found when arguments turn into who is right and who is wrong or who is good and terrible. It comes down to the choice: which story you choose to adopt? I recommend letting love rule.

REAL-LIFE STORY AND APPLICATION #2

Love, Marriage, House Project, and Money: The Perfect Storm

Money can be one of the most stressful conversations for couples. Our money stories go deep and are so emotionally charged, as I mentioned in Chapter 1 when discussing the money story that one of our podcast participants had, which is a big reason couples avoid any conversation around money. I can't tell you how often I give couples homework to discuss finances, and they either put it off for weeks or never get to it. It's challenging enough that we have our own money stories and now combine them with someone else's. But it's crucial to address these challenges, as doing so can lead to a healthier financial communication.

I will share a personal story about a money conflict with my husband to show how deep and robust conflict or conversations around money can get. Thanks to the Layers of Stories Technique, we grew even closer after our argument, though it did go dark for a bit.

I trust you will be able to relate to some of the insights we gained through the process. I hope you will take it with you and set aside a time to pause and explore all of your own stories around money. Exchange them with your partner to illuminate and move beyond them as individuals and as a couple. This process is healing and powerful. You'll see.

A little background: My husband and I live in a small, charming, 100-year-old farmhouse cottage. We had set a budget for our kitchen improvements, and I was excited as I love to cook and have dreamed of a farmhouse/country cottage kitchen for many years. My biggest thing is having it be functional and intuitive; everything has its place right where you need it. Storage is limited in our cozy space, so I suggested we create a pantry in the entryway. My suggestion did not go over well, and when I saw what I interpreted as his stress and heard his concern over my "project creeping," I imploded and exploded simultaneously. Step #1 of the Layers of Stories Technique needed to be employed.

TIME OUT: PAUSE.

Fortunately, we came around to doing the technique separately and then together. Did we have a couple of difficult days in between? I know for me, I went dark and catastrophic. As I have mentioned, sometimes the darkness holds the lessons for us to illuminate. We must go gently through the steps with patience, compassion, and curiosity. (You know the drill by now.)

When I used this technique alone, the unearthed stories were layered and convoluted; I am not lying. Talk about worth. Talk about family history. Talk about my family legacy stories around money. It took my husband and I a few days to come back together about this. I recommend waiting until you are in a space where you can remain neutral and compassionate toward yourself and each other as best as possible. Again, use a "time out" to go inward for a calm, constructive conversation with more clarity and less emotional charge. He did not understand why I was so upset. I accused him of having a bad relationship with money while I got lower and lower for not having all of the money to pay for it. Let me break down each side here, and I will share the beautiful growth and insights that occurred after we came back together and used this technique. You can also see these broken down on the sample worksheet accompanying this technique.

Stories I discovered I was carrying about myself:
- "I can only do this project alone and with my money because that is the only way I will have my creative expression and not be bound by my husband's fear around money and his need to be the boss." (*FEAR*)

- "I am not meant to have the material things I want in this life." (*FEAR*)

- "My life is more about giving than receiving." (*FEAR*)

- "I won't have a home that has a piece of my creative expression." (*FEAR*)

- "I did not come from money and I'm embarrassed about that and full of shame and unworthiness." (*FEAR*)

Stories I assumed and projected that my husband was carrying:
- "My husband prefers a wife that has money and will go along with whatever he wants." (*FEAR*)

- "My husband is burdened and stressed by this and only wants to do it because I want it." (*FEAR*)

- "My husband does not think I know how to save and handle money."

(*FEAR*)

- "My husband is afraid of project creep and that this is going to cost a fortune." (*FEAR*)

I don't know how these stories are landing for you. Are you surprised? Can you relate? Are they far-fetched? Whatever your thoughts and judgments are, I am telling you that these were the stories beneath my patterns of pursuing a sabotaging disagreement with my husband simultaneously, distancing myself even more and more from him.

In the few days I sat with these stories on my own before hearing my husband's side and his stories, I experienced two very important "other factors" (found in Step #5). These factors not only enlightened me but also helped my husband have more compassion and understanding of why my emotions were so intense when we had our above argument.

One epiphany concerned my family's money legacy. I uncovered layers that involved memories of my father appearing stressed about money and my, as a child, not wanting my father to feel that stress. When I brought up this potential entryway pantry, and my husband appeared stressed, I felt the same need to fix it. I did not want him to feel overwhelmed by money like I'd witnessed my father. So now we have my Fixer Part on the scene to ensure everything is okay for everyone involved. And Fixer Part got together with a Saboteur Part and thought, well, if I move away to a separate place, he won't have to deal with any of this. After all, what amount of worth do I possess if I cannot pay for this whole project solely on my own? There's that worthiness theme again. (Keep your eye out for that—the Saboteur Part often carries stories of unworthiness). And yes, these were the stories and thoughts I was having.

Another memory came up during this time of introspection—a memory related to feeling a sense of being home. My parents moved from my childhood home when I was a sophomore in college and moved around a lot, so I did not feel a sense of roots for almost all of my young adult life, and it is something that I crave now in my mid-life. Being a part of this kitchen planning project would help me feel roots in a home that was not only my husband's childhood home but also the home he shared with his first wife.

These two epiphanies would not have come had I not taken the time to do this work and technique. You can imagine how the two traumatic memories and themes in my life contributed to our intense argument. Moreover, as a result of this time of introspection and my new understanding, I was better, calmer, and enlightened before meeting with my husband to perform Step #5, exchanging our stories. I felt like some of these stories I uncovered in the Layers of Stories Technique were now healed. I could look at them with wonder and compassion rather than having them sneak out in a catastrophic fight-or-flight or freeze response with my husband. Fixer Part and Saboteur Part could step back and let us have a constructive conversation. When I met with my husband and we did this together (about 5 days later by the way), we learned so much!

Are you ready for it?

First, he shared with me the stories he was holding for himself and for me:

- He is afraid he will run out of money in retirement. (*FEAR*)

- He worries that I (Jen) won't save enough or make savings a priority for my future. (*FEAR*)

- He thinks I am going to blow the budget and project creep and does not want to spend more than the budget on it and does not want me (Jen) to spend her money on it. (*FEAR/LOVE*)

- He is afraid that we may not agree on what needs to be prioritized or what is most important. (*FEAR*)

Our lessons learned and how we are even stronger because of this technique:
We discovered that every story was based on fear, except for the one where my husband did not want me to spend any of my money because he wanted me to save, which was a loving gesture. FEAR: False Evidence Appearing Real.

Could we find some truth appearing real in each one of those stories? Yes. But neither of us would want to be pinned into a box labeled with that story, and neither of us would want that story (or its Parts involved) to guide our kitchen renovation, our relationships with money, our future, or our marriage. Though some of my assumptions of HIS stories were accurate, they are still not stories we want to be ruled by. We do not wish to view our reality through the lens of those stories.

What my husband discovered in this process demonstrates the power of taking the time to do this technique for your relationships.

He expressed this:

I could have predicted your first story and all the stories you projected on me. However, the ones that follow about you not being meant to have nice things or that I would judge you and your worth by how much money you or your family had makes me very sad. I do not feel that way and do not want you to think I feel that way; I want these stories to be healed.

Can you feel the healing of that interaction? Did that make us even more connected as a couple? If you answered yes, you are correct.

My husband also said that more than ever, he wanted me to feel rooted in this home and that I was a part of its creative expression in the most important room for me: the kitchen.

In conclusion, do not just think about this technique; do it, use it, and implement it. You can do this alone or with a therapist if you are struggling. My husband and I went on to collaborate and co-create a beautiful kitchen with only a couple of very, very small arguments, which were mostly around exhaustion and displacement and not around money and stories. We were pleasantly surprised that many of the fear stories were false and did not continue through the process. I had even forgotten what the stories were. We both love our new kitchen, and I feel more like a part of this house than ever. The harmony we experienced resulted from this technique. I am so grateful we did not let the sabotaging stories lead the way.

I've been using this technique with couples in my practice, and it is so rewarding to see the compassion they build and the bonding they experience as a result of doing this healing work.

Quick and final note: You may have noticed that my husband has a substantial Financial Planner Part. In my work with couples, it's more often than not that one partner has a strong Financial Part, and the other partner does not. This dynamic usually causes a lot of frustration and confusion unless you invest in healing work like the Layers of Stories Technique to help it all make sense.

REAL-LIFE STORY AND APPLICATION #3

How Shame Responses Can Destroy a Beautiful Friendship

Before describing this example of using the Layers of Stories Technique, let's talk about Shame Responses beginning with yet another powerful quote by Brené Brown:

> Shame, blame, disrespect, betrayal, and withholding affection damage the roots from which love grows. Love can only survive these injuries if they are acknowledged, healed, and rare.

It's time to talk about shame, and who else but Dr. Brené Brown should we turn to? She has done extraordinary research on shame, and I find her work profound and influential. She is taking us all to better places. Shame is usually a component of the "not enough" stories we have discussed. When we combine a shame response with a shame story, it is hard to discern what is real at all.

If we become more self-aware of our shame and what our shame responses look like and then illuminate our shame stories with compassion using the Layer of Stories Technique, the shame stories and responses will lose their power over us. So, together, let us learn more. Brené Brown speaks of three reactions to shame. When we are embarrassed or ashamed, there is the potential to respond in one of the three following ways:

- Move away or isolate

- Move toward or over-apologize

- Move against or attack and make the other person feel blame and shame

Dr. Linda Hartling is the original writer of these shame responses, and Brené brought the lessons home for us.

Here is a personal story to help demonstrate this combination of shame stories and shame responses while also showing my application of the Layers of Stories Technique.

Background: It is October 2021. Covid has become less of a concern than it was, but it is still unsettling, and the vaccine is causing much debate. Our country and society have made it political, and there is a divide that covers a large spectrum that spreads from the belief that "everyone should be vaccinated" to "nobody should be vaccinated." Three special people join me at my dining room table for a meal. Each person demonstrates a person somewhere on that vaccination spectrum. One of us (me) believes it is a personal choice to get vaccinated, and I had chosen to do so, though it was hard considering my autoimmune symptoms. Another person is trying to protect their family and friends, especially children, and believes everyone should be vaccinated. Their opinion around this is passionate. One person admits that they had COVID-19 6 or 7 months prior and their body fought it, so they, at the moment, are not vaccinated. Another person had undergone cancer treatment and was in remission and did not want to change the balance of their system with some new vaccine. Finding out that two people were not vaccinated caused the person at the table who believed everyone should be vaccinated to turn to a state of fear and concern and no longer sit at our table; they are now standing. There then ensued a debate on statistics. Any joy or connection felt minutes before had completely dissolved. I excuse myself to go to the bathroom. I am in my bathroom staring in the mirror, miserable that this has happened, but I haven't said a single word up to this point. I take a deep breath and decide what I am going to do.

I returned to the scene and reflected on each person's stance regarding the vaccination and their journey or "Why." That part was neutral. I simply reflected on and restated each person's personal beliefs.

I then shared how I wish this debate had not happened. I expressed how angry and upset I was that the discussion had turned to judgment and contention. It felt like we were a microcosm of society, and the division that escalated during this time was because of COVID-19, vaccination, and its relation to politics. One of the special people who believes everyone should be vaccinated proceeds to exit my home abruptly. I walk them out, and the shame stories and responses begin or continue, depending on how you view them.

My overall shame story was, "I jeopardized their family by having them over without confirming everyone's vaccination status."

I employ the "moving toward" shame response. On my front lawn, I begin apologizing, feeling sorry that I hadn't thought to inform them that there would be people unvaccinated in attendance and that there would be people with such different stances on the topic. I feel ashamed—the guilt is: "Did I handle this okay?" The shame is: "I am bad because I didn't give full transparency around vaccination status." Is this a new social custom that everyone should be doing? Inform everyone about who is vaccinated and who isn't before they come to your home.

I remember also feeling shame for the people at the table who weren't vaccinated and their positions. I felt guilty for our society because we'd become so divided on this topic, and my dining room was just a microcosm. This "move toward" shame response continued as I woke up the next morning after only three hours of sleep because this was so upsetting. I sent an apologetic text for my oversight, wishing her and her family good health. There was no response to that text.

Then, "moving away" kicked into full gear. This shame response is when you want to isolate yourself as a result of feeling ashamed. Stories swirled. Was it this situation that broke our friendship? How? I thought the foundation of our friendship was strong based on a decade of loving gestures and unconditional support toward one another on a regular basis. I did not want to talk to anyone about this. I just wanted to bury it inside, ashamed about the whole experience and this is when the stories that *I assumed* and projected onto the friend that left abruptly that night and felt so strongly about everyone should be vaccinated started to become illuminated.

Note: At the time that I'm writing this. I have never had the chance to check these stories out with the person that left my house so upset. I have no idea what stories they held, so this is just me assuming what they thought of us and why they left and never spoke to me in the same way again:

- "The people in attendance are stupid and ignorant for not being vaccinated."

- "The friendship is over because this was all too hurtful."

- "This situation that I caused is unforgivable."

So, these stories fed the desire to "move away" and isolate. Though I did reach out with a congratulatory text and card when something monumental happened in their lives and invited them to something enormous in my life, they only responded to my congratulations with a thank you. Their response to my invitation is what I would call a goodbye. To date, our friendship is different from before this happened.

What is so challenging is that when we do not know someone else's side of the story, we can create our own for them. I did have stories that fall under the "moving against" shame response. When we move against it, we use shame on shame. We try to shame the people that we think are shaming us. Two wrongs do not make a right. I'm not proud of these stories that I'm mentally attacking this person with. Deep down, I know their reasoning is not simple and black and white like my accusations below. Still, they cross my mind occasionally. These "move against" shame stories were:

- The person who is shaming us is a hurtful, narrow-minded human.

- To have our friendship break over this means they did not value our decade-long friendship anyway. What was the friendship worth to them if it could break so easily? What kind of friend are they anyway?

See? Shame on shame. It's so sad that this happens way too often, and without reconciliation, nobody can better understand what happened, heal, mend, or grow the relationship.

For all I know, they have shame stories; their distance is their shame response. The dissolution of this friendship still haunts me. Fortunately, the illumination work I did within myself and with trusted experts helped me to heal. Nobody became ill or contracted COVID-19 as a result of the event, yet so much was "infected," and we still do not know why. These stories plagued for at least two years after it occurred. I remember reflecting on that evening and seeing the pattern of fear turning into judgment, shame, and hate—in the blink of an eye. Judgment, shame, and hate can be turned inward, like in the moving away response, and stir up depression and self-loathing thoughts, or all of it can be turned against, blasting other people with this icky, judgmental, blaming, and shaming energy. Or moving away where you isolate and let it stand between you and the world.

This is how the perfect storm of shame stories and shame responses spreads like a typhoon in your inner system and in relationships. I feel as though judgment and shame can be poisonous. They mean well and try to make sure we have a good moral compass or that we can be the best we can be, but in the blink of an eye, if not watched carefully with gentleness and compassion—WHACK! We are knocked out, disillusioned by a death sentence.

Thankfully, we can calm these shame and judgment typhoons before they destroy us and our relationships. Brené Brown encourages us to voice our shame to a trusted person. Brené exclaims that when shame is voiced and met with empathy, it cannot survive, and healing occurs.

May we all practice this Layers of Stories Technique and increase our self-awareness around how the shame/hate cycle may appear. This book is a tool to help us step forward in that direction. And if it comes up in relationships, I encourage you to communicate and check out your stories with one another. In this case, I have not had the opportunity to talk it out with the person it happened with; however, taking the time to do the Layers of Stories Technique on my own and bringing it to my trusted therapist helped reduce its hold on me.

After this journal prompt, you will find another tool: a worksheet to guide you through the Layers of Stories Technique. Keep it handy for the next time you experience a heated discussion or argument. Again, whether done alone or with someone else, you will find it useful.

Journal Prompt: Do you have an event in your life that has left you with shame stories you have kept hidden? If yes, write/voice it here, find a trusted and empathetic person, therapist, or friend, and share it with them.

The Layers of Stories Technique

There is likely a story when we are feeling a heightened emotion in conflict. It is also likely that the story is not entirely true. Holding onto these stories and hiding them can mire us in confusion, hurt, and resentment. This technique aims to provide steps that will help you clear up any misunderstandings or deep-seated beliefs that are not helpful. This tool allows you to illuminate beneficial lessons from intense emotions and heated conflict. Its purpose is to bring healing to each layer and ensure the layers of stories are not getting in the way of healing and mending a healthy and fulfilling relationship.This worksheet can be used on its own. If you would like more understanding around this technique, check out Chapter 4.

Premise: You have a heated disagreement or conflict with someone in your life: a partner, friend, colleague, etc., as evidenced by a fight-flight-freeze response, withdrawal or distancing, defensiveness, and an emotional charge.

Step #1: Take a time-out. Separate and go to a safe and calming place. Bring a pen and this worksheet.

Step #2a: During your time apart, engage in self-reflection with gentle curiosity and compassion. Use the chart below to write down the stories or beliefs you hold about this conflict. Fill in the first block with your stories (partner #1) or the stories you are holding about yourself and the other person. Remember, these are your perceptions, your truths. Use the samples provided from the *Love, Marriage, House Project* example for guidance, if needed.

Step #2a: Your Stories
The stories you're holding about yourself and the other person

-
-
-

Step #2a Sample: Your Stories
Jen's Stories

- I can only do this kitchen project alone and with my own money—that's the only way I will have my creative expression and not be bound by my husband's fear around money and his need to be the boss.

- I am not meant to have the material things that I want in this life.

- My life is more about giving than receiving.

- I won't have a home that has a piece of my creative expression.

- I didn't come from money and I'm embarrassed about that, and full of shame and unworthiness.

Step #2a Sample: Your Stories
Jen's Husband's Stories

- *I could run out of money in retirement.*
- *I worry that Jen won't save enough or make saving a priority for the future.*
- *I fear that Jen will blow the budget and the project will end up costing lots more than we budgeted for.*
- *I'm afraid that we may not agree on the priorities of the project and what is most important.*

Step #2b: Also while separate, fill in the block below for the other person's stories, or all of the stories *you think or are assuming* the other person is holding about you, themselves, or the situation. Use the samples below for guidance and reference if needed.

Step #2b: Other Person's Stories
The stories you think the other person is holding about the situation

-

-

-

Step #2b Sample: Other Person's Stories
Stories I thought my husband was holding

- *My husband prefers a wife that has money and will go along with whatever he wants.*

- *My husband is burdened and stressed by this kitchen renovation and only wants to do it because I want to.*

- *My husband thinks I don't know how to save and handle money.*

- *My husband thinks I "project creep" and this will cost a fortune.*

Step #3: Revisit your list in Step #2 and review each of your stories. Next to each story, write and underline either **LOVE** or **FEAR** based on where the story is coming from. So, if the story is fear-based, write **FEAR** and if it's based in love, write **LOVE**. See samples below.

Step #3 Sample: Love or Fear
Jen's Stories

- I can only do this kitchen project alone and with my own money—that's the only way I will have my creative expression and not be bound by my husband's fear around money and his need to be the boss. **FEAR**

- I am not meant to have the material things that I want in this life. **FEAR**

- My life is more about giving than receiving. **FEAR**

- I won't have a home that has a piece of my creative expression. **FEAR**

- I didn't come from money and I'm embarrassed about that, and full of shame and unworthiness. **FEAR**

Step #3 Sample: Love or Fear
Jen's Husband's Stories

- I could run out of money in retirement. **FEAR**

- I worry that Jen won't save enough or make saving a priority for the future. **FEAR/LOVE**

- I fear that Jen will blow the budget and the project will end up costing lots more than we budgeted for. **FEAR**

- I'm afraid that we may not agree on the priorities of the project and what is most important. **FEAR**

Step #4 (optional): If you are familiar with Internal Family Systems or Parts Work, revisit the list in Step 2 and name the Part you think that story comes from.

Step #4 Sample: Adding the Part that is telling the story

- I can only do this kitchen project alone and with my own money—that's the only way I will have my creative expression and not be bound by my husband's fear around money and his need to be the boss. **FEAR** Victim/Exile

- I am not meant to have the material things that I want in this life. **FEAR** Victim/Martyr

- My life is more about giving than receiving. **FEAR** Martyr

- I won't have a home that has a piece of my creative expression. **FEAR** Victim/Martyr

- I didn't come from money and I'm embarrassed about that, and full of shame and unworthiness. **FEAR** Shame/Exile

Step #5: Take a moment to fill in the box below with other factors that may have contributed to the argument. Any other information that could be related to a heated conflict or misunderstanding include:

- Defensiveness
- Blame
- Lack of sleep or lack of self-care
- Outside stressors that you and the other party may be dealing with
- Hunger
- Alcohol or substance influences

- Societal stories or norms
- Generational trauma
- Hormones
- Cultural or sub-cultural differences
- Prejudices based on socioeconomic status, ethnic backgrounds, political and religious viewpoints, sexual orientation and gender identity, or age
- A childhood wound or traumatic event from the past that feels similar to this experience

Step #5: Other Factors
Other things that may have contributed to the argument

-
-
-

Step #5 Sample: Other Factors
Other things that may have contributed to the argument

- *Generational trauma*
- *Family legacy stories and wounds*
- *Defensiveness*
- *Prejudices around socioeconomic status (both low and high)*

Step #6: If the person you argued with has done this process and has agreed to check out your stories with one another, choose a time when you are both in a calm and neutral place where you can hold compassion and curiosity within yourself for both you and the other person.
Note: Even if the person is unwilling to have a conversation, you will still gain something by doing the previous steps on your own.

In cases where you do decide to meet, here are my tips to help support a healing and constructive conversation. **Please see my resource section at the back of this book for helpful agreements and listening and speaking skills, and use it as a guide for this conversation.**

Tips:

- **Embrace the practice of active listening**. Begin by deciding who will speak first and set a timer for 10-15 minutes. During this time, the first person shares their thoughts while the other person focuses solely on listening. The listener's role is not to judge, defend, or apologize excessively but to truly hear the speaker's perspective. This exercise allows each of you to express your feelings, experiences, and concerns, *fostering a deeper understanding and empathy in your relationship.*

- **Remember that they are just stories.** Yes, maybe there is some truth in them; however, most of them come from hurt, childhood wounds, trauma, etc. Our goal is **not** to find out who is right or wrong here, or whose fault it is: our goal is to *illuminate the stories that are binding the relationship* so that those limiting beliefs can dissolve and set you free. Together, you can choose a story that is healthier and more constructive for your relationship.

- **Treat the other person and their stories the way you want you and your stories to be treated.**

- **When expressing your thoughts or feelings, consider using 'I' statements.** Try Brene Brown's "The story in my head is..." or, "I felt that you held a story that was. . ." This approach allows you to share your perceptions without placing blame or making assumptions, fostering a more open and non-confrontational dialogue.

If you need more guidance in having a conversation like this, consider consulting a couples therapist who can be a neutral facilitator.

Frequently Asked Questions for this Technique:

Isn't it better to just avoid difficult and uncomfortable conversations like this?

Not talking about something can make a relationship more and more unhealthy.

Think about the last time you avoided a conversation like this: did you experience silent treatments, distancing from the other person, passive aggression, or stalled relationship growth after avoiding the conversation? Having these conversations will not only help your relationship become deeper and healthier, but it will also help break through some of the discomforts you are trying to avoid, making communication more and more comfortable as you face the discomfort and practice effective communication. Even without a resolution, you will still feel clearer and better after trying to communicate.

What if we do not have time to do this technique? Is there a quicker tool that can work and still be effective?
I'm so glad you asked! *The Story in My Head* hack by Brene Brown is a quick and incredibly effective tool for all relationships. It's a surefire way to check out the story you are imagining in your head with the other person. Brene Brown advises us to say the following whenever we are ruminating or having a strong response to what someone said and there is a chance we misunderstood or misinterpreted it: *The story I'm making up is. . .*

Looking back on every story I shared in this chapter, we could have inserted this hack. For example, I could have checked out with my husband: *"The story I'm making up is you wish I were rich."* Another example is when I could have checked in with the friend who left my dining room table when other people were not vaccinated: *"The story I'm making up is you think I'm an awful friend for having you here without giving the vaccination breakdown. I'm awful for even being associated with people not vaccinated."*

Do both parties have to participate?
This technique works best when both partners participate. It is still beneficial for just one person. The entity of the relationship goes even deeper in the healing process if both parties have a chance to increase awareness and can understand one another better, so try to get both parties involved. If it doesn't work out that way, do it yourself, alone. You will find results that way, too, which is guaranteed!

How do I bring this up to my partner, friend, colleague or family member?
If you are reading this and you and a loved one or colleague are NOT in conflict, it's the perfect time to bring this technique up. You could say, *"I read this cool technique in a book, and I would like you to read about it, too. That way, the next time we get into an argument or have a conflict; we can have this helpful tool ready*

to use". If you have learned about this and have discussed it **before** anything contentious has happened, you have a solid tool to implement. Talk about it while still in a neutral and learning place—you will be golden.

What are ways I can start a conversation with someone about using this tool?

These can be applied to a partner, colleague, family member or friend:

- "Sometimes it feels easier to avoid difficult conversations, but our relationship means a lot to me, and talking about this will help us grow together even more. I know a tool/technique that helps us work through the conversation step by step. Would you be willing to try it?"

- "I want us to work together more effectively. Would you be willing to try this tool/technique that I learned about that will help us understand each other more?"

- "We keep having the same argument repeatedly; let's try this Layers of Stories Technique and see how we can interrupt this pattern so we don't keep exhausting ourselves and instead understand what is underneath this situation/argument/pattern more. What do you say we give it a try?"

- "I think I am having a hard time communicating; therefore, it's easy to misunderstand me in this conversation. I read about a tool that helps people communicate more clearly and effectively. Would you try it with me and see what happens?"

Do you recommend using this technique through text communication?

It may be helpful to suggest using this technique through a text or email, with a link or screenshot of the steps, but having the actual heart-to-heart is strongly recommended to be done in person. If in-person is not an option, it is also strongly advised to do it over the phone, Facetime or the Internet, where a back-and-forth and the ability to see body language and facial expressions are also strongly recommended.

Are there times when this method or tool is <u>not</u> recommended?

As mentioned repeatedly, you can ALWAYS do this technique by yourself, and I know the process will bring you more insight and understanding. So, it would never be the case that the technique is NOT recommended for healing, learning, and growing on your own.

However, sometimes, doing this technique with someone else is not recommended. These are those times:

- Someone is not willing to participate. Respect that boundary if they openly refuse to use this technique.

- Someone no longer wants to be in a relationship with you. If they have made that clear and taken the time to decide to end the relationship, it's better to honor that boundary than keep pushing for it and suggesting they use this technique.

- Neither you nor your partner are in a neutral place. In other words, if you or someone is hijacked by a Part, like Anger or Defensiveness, and in the need of making something right or wrong/black or white or some sort of blame game, then you are NOT in a rational place. If there is rigidity and one or more parties are standing firm in one version of a side or story, it may bring on more pain to try and break it down with them. It could keep the conversation in an ineffective, destructive loop. If and when that happens, you can always decide it is not the right time and suggest you do it when there is the shared goal of constructive growth. You want to be in a place where you can speak for your Parts, not from your Parts. For the story, not from the story. A neutral place open to hearing and understanding multiple perspectives and sides is necessary.

- You or the other person is feeling a lot of shame, and there is a strong shame response involved. (Real Life Story #3 talks about this.) Before you do this technique, bring the shame into light (remember, shame can not survive in illumination, empathy, and compassion), and once you feel that those shame parts are calm, revisit using this technique.

- If you try to have this conversation or other healthy conversations and you have not been able to have a safe or rational conversation, if they respond by turning it all back on you and blaming you or using another form of manipulation, just stop and accept that you will not be able to have a healthy and constructive conversation.

- If you are moving toward a goal/dream and part of you is clear, but you're still experiencing some doubt and hesitation, it's not a good time to use this technique. Other people's stories or doubts could persuade you. Refrain from engaging in conversations where someone wants to go through their layers of stories in order to convice you not to step toward your dream because of their own critical, limiting, doubting, and fearful stories.

Final Notes on the Layer of Stories Technique

This technique gives us a step-by-step method to evaluate a conversation from all angles with introspection, awareness, and transparency. We can take the lessons from a difficult discussion or disagreement. Through this technique, we can empower ourselves to choose the healthiest and most constructive story for the relationship. I'm not suggesting we push anything under the rug. With all of the illumination, that is impossible. The information derived from this technique allows you to choose a path where the fear-based stories and false beliefs are not in charge of the relationship.

Again, this technique will always be valuable for you to do on your own. It will increase self-awareness, connection, and self-understanding, which can only bring good things to your life and relationships. Still, in the blessed opportunities you have where you can have a healthy and practical application of this technique with someone in your life, your relationship will grow exponentially.

CHAPTER 5

❋

Stories From Others, Stories We Give Others

Whenever you start doubting yourself, whenever you feel afraid, just remember: Courage is the root of change—and change is what we're chemically designed to do. So when you wake up tomorrow, make this pledge: No more holding yourself back. No more subscribing to others' opinions of what you can and cannot achieve. And no more allowing anyone to pigeonhole you into useless categories of sex, race, economic status and religion. Do not allow your talents to lie dormant, ladies. Design your own future. When you go home today, ask yourself what you will change. And then get started.
~ Bonnie Garmus, *Lessons in Chemistry*

In this chapter, we look closer at when someone else places a story on us, which we then adopt. We will also look at when someone says something about us that supports a story we already have about ourselves, as well as when we are the ones that place a story on someone else, otherwise known as gossip.

When We Adopt a Story that Someone Else Put on Us

Parents, teachers, counselors, coaches, therapists, mentors, and bosses all have a big responsibility: watching what limiting beliefs or stories they plant in the brains of those under their guidance. No pressure. We all mean well. And I'm sure one of our Protector Parts is trying to make sure we keep the other person safe and not feel any hardship or discomfort. Still, we must be mindful of what kind of messaging we're giving. When we project a limiting belief on someone else, they may take it on as fact and create a story that keeps them from pursuing something that brings them joy. "You can't do…" Fill in the blank. What feels like a short comment can have a long-lasting impact.

Whether sports, academics, the arts, or other career paths, a message could trap someone into doing something they don't want to do. These comments often happen in creative and expressive arts, which breaks my heart. Many people will say an art teacher told them they can't draw. A chorus teacher told them they couldn't sing. Again, they mean well. They probably think they're doing the student a favor by guiding them into a different field. Therein lies the problem: the arts are not just a career path. They are a way to heal, expand, innovate, and solve problems. Song, dance, painting, poetry, writing, theater, and all of the arts have been around for centuries across all cultures as a form of healing, growth, and transformation. Somewhere along the line in our society, it has become something only the trained should pursue.

For those of you reading this who are like me and can be susceptible to other people's stories and opinions of you, I strongly recommend that you take the time to do the Layers of Stories Technique or use another technique to discern what comes from *your* heart and not someone else's fear. Their opinion might stem from their own family of origin, past, inner critic, or trauma. Wayne Dyer used to say, "When someone shares their opinion, simply respond: 'Thank you for your opinion.'" He believes that is all it is: their opinion.

Beyond the arts, people can project other destructive stories onto us, like their opinions about our looks, our intellect, our gifts, our joys, our personalities. It is extremely important that we do not live our lives for others and the stories that they are projecting onto us. It is important that we do the work to connect with our authentic selves so that we can get clearer about who we are and what we want. As a result, when someone else tries to project their fearful stories on us and our journey, we will not feel like we need to defend ourselves and we do not feel like we need to live according to their opinions. Choose love. Choose a life connected to your authentic self and what is healthiest and best for you and your life. Remember, the power to choose your authentic self is in your hands, which can lead to a more fulfilling and empowered life.

When Someone Reinforces a Limiting Story that You Already have of Yourself

Another way limiting stories can catch fire within us and burn down our dreams is when someone reinforces a story *we already have.* The following story moved me to tears during one of my Illuminating the Stories that Bind Us workshops.

A participant shared how her story since her childhood has been that she never makes it to the elusive bar or standard that her family set up for her. She is a successful, well-sought-after medical professional with her practice. She lives in an elite town. She has two children. Now, picture this moment: she has a graduation party for her daughter. Everyone is in her gorgeous backyard, overlooking the water. Caterers are going by, offering appetizers. Her cousin strolls up to her and says, "Do you ever feel bad that you haven't taken your life any further than you have?" Her heart and jaw dropped. The other participants and I at the workshop began validating the participant's hurt and confusion. We all tried to reassure her that what her cousin said to her had more to do with him, his Parts, and his stories. His fear. His pressure. His protection. His thoughts and definitions around status, success, and achievement.

Still, this participant cannot help but play that out in her head. It only confirmed the story and limiting belief that goes on inside of her. But anyone on the outside can see that she has gone above and beyond in her life. Even she can see that. I think I speak for most people when I say it takes a lot for us not to allow what someone else says to define us. Don Miguel Ruiz talks about this in his book, *The Four Agreements*, with profound wisdom. Ruiz advises us not to take what someone else says personally. Why? Because by the time someone expresses something to us, their opinion has traveled through their history and stories before it reaches our ears.

I wish the participant in the story above and her cousin could employ the Layers of Stories Technique from the previous chapter. I recommend you try it whenever you are experiencing an interaction that produces an emotional charge like the one above. And what a gift if the other person is willing to do it too. However, we do not have control over that, so empower yourself by doing it yourself.

Why Do We Gossip and Project Stories onto Others?

If telling ourselves stories isn't bad enough, creating stories about others can be just as damaging. I know nearly everyone does this, and my intent is not to shame us, but to enlighten and give us that pause. In the Disney movie *Bambi*, the character Thumper so sweetly exclaims while twirling his foot, "If you can't say something nice, don't say nothing at all." Imagine a world where we could do this. I do not know a soul who feels good when they hear someone speak poorly about them behind their back.

There are plenty of sayings out there: *"Who cares what other people think?"* *"Sticks and stones may break my bones, but names will never hurt me." "Don't take it personally." "Their opinion is their opinion."* And more.

As much as we try to internalize all of the above wisdom, as much as we try not to talk about other people, and as much as we try not to let it bother us that other people talk about us, it haunts us to some extent.

So, let us illuminate the reasons why people criticize and gossip. In the book *Daring Greatly*, Brené Brown discusses her research with critics. Some of the themes that she cites are related to this section:

- People are hard on each other because they are hard on themselves: people judge and criticize others on the things that they are most judgmental and critical about within themselves.

- Competition: we feel most vulnerable about what we are most critical about.

- We judge people who are vulnerable to shame because *we* are so susceptible to shame.

When I take a closer look at why I gossip, most of the time, it is all about me. Whether it is to make myself feel better, or to process some emotional reaction inside of me, those reasons are more about me than the other person. These are some of the specific examples that my gossip usually boils down to:

- When I feel hurt or attacked, sharing that with other people and getting their sympathy soothes and validates me.

- I feel guilty or "not enough" about something, so if I can rationalize it or say something about someone else, it is an attempt to alleviate the guilt.

- I feel threatened in some way, so saying something about the person I feel threatened by gives me a false sense of power.

- They are bumping against one of the stories I have about myself that I am trying to change, and I feel challenged by them.

- They have triggered a Part of me that still has an emotional charge.

- They have crossed a boundary they don't know I have set because I haven't told them about it.

I am sure there are more examples. The bottom line is that gossip is more of a reflection of us and our Parts. It is more about what is happening within us than about the person we gossip about. Again, this is not to shame us. It's to better understand yourself by illuminating where we hold ourselves back. By doing so, we can help ourselves and others unbind.

I have been trying a mental trick: whenever I notice myself judging in my mind or about to say something poor about someone else, I say to myself, "Clean slate," and I give that person a clean slate—offering an opportunity where they are not receiving any stories thrown at them, telepathically, psychically or otherwise. We all deserve a clean slate. A chance to have a fresh start, reinvent ourselves, renew, and be any change we wish to make. May we free ourselves and others by using the clean slate method before we judge ourselves, say anything damaging about ourselves, and judge and say something terrible about someone else. Everyone deserves the room to change into something else.

Closing Thoughts on Not Taking on Someone Else's Story of Us and Being Mindful of Gossip

- Pause before telling someone they can or can't do something, and ensure you deliver something constructive and helpful.
- Next time you notice a judgment in your mind about yourself or someone else, try the "clean slate" tool.
- When someone delivers a message to you that is crushing and stomps on your spirits, consider whether the message was more about their fears/ protection.
- When someone says, "You always…" or "You never…," that is usually a signal that it's coming from a Part. We're too dynamic as humans to do something all the time, every time. Look more closely at the comment and discern whether it is fruitful to consider.
- When a comment, opinion, or judgment feels starkly opposite to your interpretation or how you felt when doing whatever was delivered, consider that it is more about them, and trust yourself.

Yung Pueblo sums it up well in an excerpt from *The Way Forward*:

"The magic happens once you accept that you can't regulate others' emotions or experiences—that's when you begin to live your most authentic life
some people will not "get" you.
but what matters is that you get you
be kind
help others
and don't forget to live for yourself."

Journal Prompt: Next time you catch yourself gossiping, take some time to reflect on it. With gentle curiosity, ask yourself: *What was my goal in saying those things about another person?* Write what comes up.

CHAPTER 6

✳

The Importance of Illuminating the Stories that Bind Us

"Pain is a warning that something is wrong."
~ Madonna

Ever feel a nudge? To me, a nudge is a wake-up call. Sometimes it is quiet, like a whisper in the ear, and other times it is loud, like an elbow to the ribs. You know that elbow nudge. It's similar to when you want your mom to stop telling the neighbor your secrets, so you give her that elbow nudge. The nudges I'm about to share here told me it was time to take a closer look at the stories binding me because they interfered with my peace, joy, and healthy relationships. Some of these nudges were emotional, some physical. Either way, they told me, *"Pay attention here; there is something you need to look at."*

These nudges or "warnings" literally pushed me toward illuminating my binding stories. Thankfully, I answered the calls, the knocks, the nudges, and the illumination transformed my life in incredibly positive ways. That is why I am determined to share this book with as many people as I can.

Here are six specific nudges. You will read how they were uncomfortable and how I was trapped. Later in this section, I include a checklist for you to see if it is time for you to illuminate your stories. I also spell out why this work is so transformative, essential, and influential in living a happier life and for the health of our relationships with self and others.

NUDGE #1

The Post-Break-Up Devastation

The first nudge came when I was around 30 years old. I was single. I was craving a relationship, a partnership. Call it biological. Call it desire. I wanted to be in a serious relationship; it had been seven years since I was in one. I was looking everywhere for this special mate. I was dating, and most dating scenarios would follow this sequence:

First, I would have some apprehensions, so I was guarded and held back. Next, there would be an explosive connection, which would quickly fade into a breakup, usually peppered with some ghosting and me pining after something long over. You may recall reading a specific example of this in Chapter One when I shared about the third episode of my podcast. These potential suitors would break through the walls of protection around my heart, and then they would initiate the breakups. The breakups fed, triggered, and confirmed whatever limiting stories I had about myself. That pattern and experience would often put me into a deep, dark, depressive episode. I would feel lost and lonely, and would stop dating entirely. And even if somewhere deep inside of me, I *knew* I had dodged a bullet with that particular suitor, the wounded part of me was devastated, and the "I am not enough" story would wreak havoc by one or more of my Parts. I was generally very happy and positive, so these dark dips were a huge contrast and would feel like a nudge that I needed to tend to. I encourage you to keep track of patterns you see and "out-of-character nudges"—they have an important message, and something needs to be voiced and listened to. These patterns are a sign that a story needs illumination.

NUDGE #2

Strong Emotional (Anxiety) Pattern

This nudge was inspired by the palpable emotional pattern of anxiety whenever I would visit my family in upstate New York. I lived in Boston but still visited my family regularly in New York, especially right after I moved from New York City to Boston. I often considered moving back to my hometown to help my sister raise my niece as she raised her independently after her divorce. I had the honor of helping my sister and niece in the early years of my niece's life. Returning to Saugerties, NY, or New York City would also bring me closer to my brother, who still lived there. I sought therapy to help me make this significant decision about where I should live. I went weekly and consistently and started to illuminate the stories around this pattern of anxiety and the need to help or fix. Therapy provided the space and opportunity to shine a light on these strong and uncomfortable emotional patterns from Nudge #2 and the emotional patterns I was experiencing in Nudge #1. The sessions helped me make more sense of these patterns, making them less in control of me.

Being able to talk about Nudge #1 and Nudge #2 and the painful emotional patterns I experienced helped me scratch the surface of the identity and stories that began around a broken heart and intense family dynamics. Stories like, *"If I don't make my family feel better, I am nothing,"* or, *"I'm not pretty, smart, or talented enough to be loved in a romantic relationship"* (from Nudge #1). At this very moment, while I'm typing these stories, I am pleased to say with complete honesty and assurance that these stories and these patterns feel so far away (thank God!) Yet, during that time, the stories and Parts that carried the stories felt front and center within my system, and there was only a slight separation from them. Talk about Parts hijacking—that feeling where you can't focus or concentrate, and the discomfort radiates through your entire body. These patterns had become so much a part of me that I could not see the stories around them, but I could certainly *feel* the nudge to my ribs. And had I not gone to therapy to help uncover the stories and illuminate them, I do not know where I would be today. Listen to those intense, repetitive emotional patterns you feel when you are around your family of origin—it's a nudge, and I guarantee there is a story that is not true lying underneath them. There is an opportunity to heal, transform the story, and have a whole new relationship with your family.

Nudge #3

No Space for a Healthy Relationship

As I continued unpacking these stories and doing my healing work of self-love, I met my now husband, and when we started dating, of course, layers of the first two nudges were still around. Fortunately, Nudge #1 and the emotional patterns around my insecurities and dating became more and more healed as I became more aware of these stories, and my relationship with myself improved. Nudge #1 also dissolved when our relationship grew in depth; I could check stories out with him (remember the hack from the last chapter?) and became more secure.

However, Nudge #2 came out loud when I was building a new and different role in my family while building a new family with this serious partner in my life. Being in a serious relationship put me in a position where I had to face these stories head-on in order for space and energy to be available for this new relationship and family. At the beginning of our relationship, this nudge came up as a conflict over me not being present in our relationship. I would be distracted trying to fix something in my family of origin. While single, this particular nudge wouldn't exist because there wasn't someone observing me and someone I needed to create space and room for when I was alone. Maybe some of my close friends would witness my shift into Fixer Part and the anxiety that came with it. However, when a partner enters your life, they have a front-row seat. They see these patterns up close and experience the impact of the patterns as well.

For example, I would be on the phone with my family for hours while he was at my apartment waiting to spend time with me. I remember working on this dynamic with my coach, Kelly Russell. She helped me dig deeper into these stories of needing to be there for my family at the expense of my new relationship. She would help me get to the core as we had these deep dive, five-hour sessions where we'd dig through layer by layer to illuminate the stories. Coach Kelly refers to them as "illusions," as she used the influential book and practice from *A Course in Miracles* to help me heal. She guided me in forgiveness work to help transform the stories as well. Those consistent little arguments you're having with your partner are a signal and nudge that there is a story in need of illumination.

NUDGE #4

The Physical Body

This message was LOUD and physical. Sometimes, our stories start to run through our bodies to a point where our bodies scream back at us with pain or illness. A few health knocks showed me that I was living out my stories on autopilot as if they were real. The mind-body connection is so accurate. Mind, Body, Soul. Emotional, Physical, and Spiritual. All very real and wise. Looking back, I must have ignored the signals of my body reflecting the stories my mind had been running for years. I could probably write a book solely on this nudge.

In 2016 and 2019, my body became inflamed. Suddenly, my wrists, knees, and shoulders swelled to the point that I felt chronic pain. I was in my mid-to-late 30s, so this arthritis was undoubtedly a warning to my doctors. They tested for rheumatoid arthritis, and the results were negative. Lupus was considered a suspect, and when my doctor told me about this potential diagnosis, my response was, "hell no!" So, I sought every holistic and alternative intervention I could. I met with psychics, astrologers, health intuitive, functional medical doctors, Western primary care physicians, therapists, and healers. I would nudge back at this nudge from every possible angle I could. These providers and healers taught me many things, and among those many things, I learned that my body was reflecting my stories. When you have autoimmune symptoms, your body thinks there is something it needs to attack, but there isn't anything, so it starts to attack your joints—hence the inflammation. My body mimicked my stories about worth and not being enough by attacking itself.

Both times I experienced a flare, I was experiencing stress or, as my mom always calls it, dis-ease. I was in survival mode, carrying stories of lack, and Martyr, Savior, and Fixer Parts were front and center. I can distinctly pinpoint stories of fear, like *"I would not be able to support myself,"* or *"I could not help or fix others in my care."* I lost a genuine connection with myself, my body, and my own needs. Instead, I lived under these stories of needing to be everything for everyone.

Our minds are so powerful. I remember Joe Dispenza once saying, *"Your body is a servant to your mind."* He often asks, *"What are you broadcasting?"* At that time, I was broadcasting that I was not as important as those around me. I invite everyone who has ever experienced a health knock to include this question in their treatment: "What is my mind broadcasting to my body?" Pause, and gently investigate these stories. Reconnect with your body from a curious and creative place rather than from autopilot and autoplay of these limiting stories.

NUDGE #5

The Suicidal Part

The last knock I will mention here was a loud and dark one that I struggle to admit, but I must be transparent and honest with you in this book. "Keeping it real," as they say, and breaking the shame and stigma around suicidal ideation, I'm going to share with you a time where my Suidical Part (I love how the approach of Internal Family Systems so effectively describes it as a Part trying to navigate unbearable feelings—so empowering).

It was a little over a year after the Covid global pandemic began. Holding a healing space for clients and managing their anxiety and exhaustion from the collective crisis started to take a toll on me. Now, I know that I genetically have a biochemical predisposition of depression that I treat holistically. So the Suicidal Part was not a complete stranger in my life. Thankfully, the Depressive Part and Suicidal Part only came around on occasion and would only stick around for a day or two at most. I usually treat it holistically and spiritually and can move through it with interventions and tools I've learned along the way. However, in that very moment, the Suicidal Part felt the closest and more in the lead than ever in my life.

On this morning when Suicidal Part was gaining the lead and working with the Depressive Part to amplify feelings of powerlessness and helplessness, I asked my husband if he would help me take my own life. My Parts were over-whelmed with many things, and I felt completely defeated. At that moment, this seemed like a solution. "Permanent solution to a temporary problem/feel-ing" is what my mom always said. You can imagine that my husband, who does not have and has never had a Suicidal Part, was confused and shocked and did not know what to do.

I had a shamanic healing appointment that day with Lisa Desrosiers, and I texted her, "*Hey, I'm in a dark space. Is it safe to go to a shamanic healing session?*" I wish I still had her exact response on my phone, but it was something to the effect of: "*This is the perfect time for a session, and often the darkness is coming up for healing.*" My sessions with Lisa during this time were rich beyond measure. I had experiences of my deceased father dressed up as Merlin, telling me it was okay to be selfish and to follow my dreams. And a beautiful, blue butterfly with wings expanding as far as they could go came and whispered the importance that I live a *fully expressed life.* I had visions of being on stage. All of these were a part of helping my subconscious heal and shift into different stories—out with the old, self-destructive stories and in with the purposeful, expansive, dream-realizing ones.

The blue butterfly was the perfect image to come to me because that is the type of transformation that was occurring and what I hope for all of you in reading this book and doing this work. Shamanic healing is an incredible way of accessing the soul language and the vast knowledge within us all. It knows what we need to hear.

I have to tell you that in the past five years of really investing in this illumi-nating the stories work, I have moved toward my dreams (a.k.a. the best an-ti-depressant ever), and my Suicidal and Depressive Parts are calm and quiet. I can't tell you the last time they took charge of my system in the ways they did before this work. *True story.*

If you have dark and loud experiences with a Depressive Part or a Suicidal

Part, that is a nudge to do this work. Shine a light on it, please. Reach out for help. Our society still tends to hide these experiences in deep, dark places. We can't work with these Parts and their stories when they are hidden deep within and covered by stories of protection. Take the nudge as a cue to turn the light on, and then you'll know what you're bumping up against.

Nudge #6

The Existential Crisis

Staying on the topic of dreams and the Covid global pandemic, many of us had an existential pause during this crisis. When things slowed down and we realized what mattered most, many of us took inventory of our lives and decided we wanted to listen to our hearts.

One of the blessings of everything going virtual was that it opened the door to reuniting with music coaches Mick and Tess Pulver, who lived many miles and states away. I worked with them in 2016, and this was an opportunity to work with them virtually in weekly coaching sessions. In the first coaching session, I shared with them my dreams of being a performer. I talked about three dreams that knocked on my heart: One dream is to be a Broadway musical actress. The second is to be an 80s cover band lead singer, and the third is singing and covering Billie Holiday and other smooth, classic artists in a jazz bar or restaurant.

It was incredibly liberating simply to state them.

It was also enlightening to realize how many stories had blocked me from singing, performing, and being on stage. **Here are a few:**

"It's selfish to want to be on stage—give someone else the spotlight."

"I need to work hard and earn money; I don't have time to do something like that."

"I'm not good enough to sing and perform."

"I'll do it in the next lifetime."

I began spending time every week singing virtually with Mick and Tess, and they would prescribe a song to help me break through my limiting beliefs. I felt alive, free, happy, and fulfilled.

I'm immensely grateful for this existential nudge. It is one of the nudges that led to this book. If you hear yourself saying things like, "Not in this lifetime," "Next lifetime," or any other phrase that pushes those dreams out of your reality, it's time to illuminate the stories keeping you from following them.

How do you know that it's time for YOU to illuminate?

It is *always* a good time to do this work. Every day, we have stories we live out or live under. All day long. So, why not look more closely at them? Why not make sure they aren't leading our lives? Here are some checklists of nudges that will help you know if it's a good time to illuminate the stories binding you.

The Post-Break-Up Devastation (Nudge #1)
- ☐ You struggle to recover after a small breakup/heartache.
- ☐ You feel anxious and ruminating about the what-ifs (*What if I didn't send that text—would we still be together?*).
- ☐ Your constant rumination of what-ifs steals your ability to enjoy peace, gratitude, and joy in the present moment.
- ☐ You have difficulty building a relationship with yourself, including hobbies, self-care, and creative expression.

Strong Emotional (Anxiety) Pattern (Nudge #2)
- ☐ You are experiencing an intense emotional pattern that distracts you from the present moment.
- ☐ You feel extreme discomfort, anxiety, shame, and sadness (a.k.a Protective and Manager Parts are working to an extreme).
- ☐ You cannot pinpoint an impending or imminent reason (e.g., grief, loss, fearful event) as to why you are feeling such intense emotions.

No Space for a Healthy Relationship (Nudge #3)
- ☐ You find yourself in a repetitive pattern of conflict and disagreements with a spouse/friend/colleague/family member.
- ☐ You create stories in your mind that portray trusted people who love you as your enemies.
- ☐ Unhealthy and unbalanced relationships consume you.

The Physical Body (Nudge #4)

- ☐ You are experiencing chronic pain or a physical ailment that cannot be accounted for a specific cause.
- ☐ You are experiencing a major life situation (e.g. death, divorce, moving, job change) or stressful circumstances and suddenly you feel certain pains that you never felt before.
- ☐ You want to do things that bring you joy but the pain is holding you back.

The Suicidal Part (Nudge #5)

- ☐ You are seeking more joy but find yourself bound, boxed-in and trapped.
- ☐ Levity and gratitude are difficult to conjure.
- ☐ You feel raw, overwhelmed and hopeless.
- ☐ You feel alone and a sense like you don't belong.

The Existential Crisis (Nudge #6)

- ☐ You feel stuck and/or you are just living on autopilot.
- ☐ You have a dream or a desire that you feel strongly in your heart but you keep coming up with excuses or stories and obstacles that get in the way.
- ☐ You are feeling unsatisfied and unfulfilled.
- ☐ You know you are not living up to your full potential and utilizing your gifts/strengths.

Check-In Quiz

1. Check-in with yourself: Can you relate to any of the above nudges? *Yes or No*

2. Which one of these answers best describes how you respond when you get a nudge that a positive change is needed?
   A. *"I'm ready to listen to these nudges, and I want to dig deeper to find the story underneath to bring it to light and transform it. Bring it on!"*

   B. *"I can relate to one or more of the nudges, but I'm afraid of what that may* *mean or do to my life. Keeping things safe and familiar feels healthiest and best for me now."*

C. *"I'm not sure I feel nudges in the first place. And the idea of digging deeper and discovering things I'm not ready to look at is frightening."*

If you chose **option A**, please proceed to the journal prompt. You are ready to move forward and dig deeper. Get ready to experience the rewards of this work, and when you read the next section, you will be even more aware of the rewards and how to face some of the bumps or obstacles you may face.

If you chose **option B**, ask your Resistant and Reluctant Parts if they're willing to step aside and allow you to try the journal prompt below. If they cooperate, please proceed to the journal prompt and, with gentleness and curiosity, discover what comes up.

If you chose **option C**, skip the journal prompt for now. Proceed to the next section of this book and see if awareness of the rewards and challenges of doing this work helps soothe and calm your fears.

Journal Prompts

1. Which one of the six nudges in this chapter could you relate to the most? Choose one that feels most disruptive in your life right now (e.g., disturbing your peace, impacting a relationship, getting in the way of a goal).

2. Describe the experience and dynamics around that nudge. Was the nudge loud? Was it a whisper? Think of everything you can around the nudge, and write your story as if you are helping a doctor understand your symptoms and patterns around this nudge.

3. Identify and write down 3-5 ineffective thoughts that you are experiencing in the patterns and dynamics around your nudge (e.g., *I always do and say things in relationships that get me in trouble*").

4. Choose the story that resonates most from the nudge. You might know because you have a feeling like, "That's it! That's the story I'm carrying." You may get tears in your eyes or feel it in your gut. Now you have identified a story that needs illumination and transformation. Nice work! Continue reading so you can learn how to break through this story.

CHAPTER 7

✳

The Rewards of Illuminating *and* Transforming Our Stories

Okay. You have identified the nudge. You know it now. You see it. You have been receiving a message asking you to look more closely at a story holding you back. And for my beloved readers who may feel hesitant or resistant around the whole nudge-and-illumination step, I commend you for sticking with this book and gathering more information. Wherever you are in this process, you are courageous! That courage has fruits to bear for your dedication. I want to share the rewards that this journey will bestow upon you. Knowing the rewards will keep you moving forward through this incredibly healing and transformative journey by knowing what you are in for.

REWARD #1

Clearing the Path of Hidden Booby Traps

When stories stay hidden, they come out "funny." They get in the way of your dreams. They cause you to be highly defensive in an argument with a loved one, or they show up as a health challenge, or you can't figure out why you stay stuck in a job or relationship that is not serving you. I have always loved this analogy: not shedding light on our stories and patterns is like walking in a room you have never been in before in complete darkness, and choosing not to turn on the light. Not knowing where the furniture is, you bump into it, maybe stubbing a toe or getting a bruise. However, if you turned on the light, you would know where the furniture is and could navigate it rather than remaining oblivious and bruised. The reward of being aware of your patterns and stories empowers you to move through situations with a clarity that puts you at an excellent vantage point where you can anticipate things, move around them with loving consciousness, and prevent unnecessary pain.

REWARD #2

Your Relationship with Yourself and Others Improves

Illuminating your stories will help you see yourself and your patterns with clarity, honesty, and discernment. This self-understanding will enhance self-connection and alignment with your mind, body, and soul. As a result of improving your self-understanding and self-awareness, you will be less apt to project stories onto others, which can often impact your relationships. The false or inaccurate stories we project onto others cause us to become increasingly distant and disconnected from others. The story takes up more and more space between us and our loved ones, colleagues, and acquaintances. Knowing and understanding yourself more increases your confidence and self-compassion and will spill over into your ability to have healthy relationships.

REWARD #3

If You Can Name It, You Can Tame It

Daniel Seigel coined this phrase, and you'll hear me say it a lot because it's so true. By naming our stories, you ignite the power to begin dissolving them. I had a client who held stories that kept her from exercising and eating well. Stories like: "I'm too old, and it's too late to make changes." When we illuminated that story and proved there were ways around it, she told me, "Jennifer, I feel like a fog has lifted." She elaborated further: "I can now see that those obstacles were just false beliefs, and for the first time in a long time, I feel a sliver of hope that I will be able to make positive changes." That's just one example of countless examples. When we can identify and name something in the way of what we really and truly want, we have the power to change it.

Reward #4

Illuminating Puts *You* in the Driver's Seat Instead of Your Limiting Stories

Our stories completely run our lives, drive our cars, and write our scripts until we shed light on them. You can understand what you really and truly want and live your life from there—aligned with the stories you *want* to run your life, not the ones that drive your car of life straight into a ditch where you get stuck.

Reward #5

Stop Detrimental Self-Fulfilling Prophecies

I encountered a quote in *Men's Magazine* by Sean Hotchkiss that eloquently captures this reward: "As long as these stories exist, we find ways to perpetuate them." This idea is also echoed by Joe Dispenza in his book, *Breaking the Habit of Being Yourself.* Based on brain science, Joe's teachings reveal how our hearts and minds collaborate and how our suffering can persist because we essentially live under a narrative of victimhood and, "why does this always happen to me?" We keep interpreting everything through that story. It's like a pathway in our brain gets established and our thought patterns keep getting stuck in the traffic of that pathway. However, it's not enough to break free from this cycle. We must actively create a new story, a new path, and begin crafting self-fulfilling prophecies that are enriching and aligned with what we really want.

Reward #6

Gain Clarity on Who or What Supports Your Best Life

When we get more precise about a belief or story that is *not* working in our lives, we start to notice what behaviors, actions, and people support the things we want, and all of the things that do *not* support it. People, places, and things. TV shows, movies, music. All of these factors in our lives and the environments we absorb regularly are essential to discern. When you illuminate, you will notice what feeds "the good wolf," as they say. You will see what factors feed you, your dreams, and your joy.

Rewards Continued *(oh yes, there are more!)*

By doing this work and transforming your story, you can create a new, more empowering story because you are putting the pen in your hands—*you* become the author. In *Change Your Story, Change Your Life*, Carl Greer writes, "Changing your story is not easy, but the payoff is considerable. You discover life is less frustrating. You experience greater love and gratitude."

Here are three more ways your life will improve due to this work:

You will live a more joyful and fulfilling life. We start living from a story we *want* instead of a story given to us, or something we feel we *should* be doing.

You will live a life better than you imagined. Another quote from Sean Hotchkiss's How to Change Your Story article: "When we dare to challenge and drop an old narrative, it is often rewritten better than we could have imagined."

Your goals and dreams are more supported. You can create stories more aligned with your heart, desires, and passion, instead of stories that misalign you.

How These Rewards Have Shown Up in My Life

These binding stories build walls between us and ourselves, our loved ones, colleagues, and our dreams. In this section, I show how the rewards of this healing journey of illumination and transformation have looked explicitly in my life in two different categories: my *relationships* and my *dreams*.

Relationships

The quality of our relationships determines our happiness more than *any other factor* (including money) in this life. This applies to all of our relationships, including our relationships with ourselves.

Relationship with Self

My relationship with myself has been so different since embarking on this journey of illuminating and breaking free from the stories that bind me. I love and appreciate myself more in so many ways. Now, when a limiting or low self-worth thought or story comes to mind, I see it and can nip it in the bud. The stories still creep in when my Doubt Part or Self-Conscious Part rises to the forefront, but my ability to catch, calm, and reintegrate them with Self-energy is profoundly different.

I feel stronger and more confident in who I am. I know who I am and who

I am not, and I am less afraid to align with those things regardless of how someone outside may respond. I know my strengths and remember that I am a star—whole, (imperfectly) perfect, and complete. I remember that others are stars, too. I live much more like I've got my own back instead of being my own worst enemy. I also think less and fear less about being someone else's enemy. I know what I bring to the table.

Relationship with My Husband
My relationship with my husband is the healthiest it has ever been. The stories in that imaginary curtain I spoke of in Chapter 4 that can block or distort the love he gives me are barely visible. Our arguments and conflicts are fewer and less intense. We can move through our disagreements with more clarity and awareness of whatever stories we may be holding or projecting on each other. And all of my underlying angst and fears of not being enough have faded, so there is only a hint of it.

As I write this, I honestly cannot remember the last time my Low Self-Worth or Trapped Exile dominated my system and our relationship. The last time my little Trapped Exile went to an extreme fight-or-flight was the kitchen remodeling argument I described in Chapter 4. I can appreciate and embrace all of the goodness our love and connection offer when my stories have been cleared and healed.

And *that* is the life I live right now. As I type this, I am so grateful for this life, him, and our marriage. When/if the stories from my Protective Parts and Exiles resurface, I will be able to navigate them consciously and lovingly.

Relationship with My Family
My relationship with my family is very different now. Whether near or far, there are fewer patterns of anxiety and panic. I used to worry about them in a way that would disturb my peace for days. Recently, a dear friend told me, "Jen, what used to take you three days to recover from or respond to only takes thirty minutes now". And she was right. I have healthier boundaries around what is mine to figure out and what is theirs. My Fixer/Martyr/Savior Parts are not in an uproar or panic about trying to fix or save. As a result, I am finding new ways to meet them with more love and less fear.

I still see myself as a good daughter/sister/aunt, even if the Fixer/Savior Parts are not hijacking. My continuous hope is that I can love them even more, appreciate them more, and judge myself (and them) less as a result of dropping the narratives that put a lot of pressure on me to fix whatever challenges they are going through. It means a lot to me to show up to my family with more peaceful and loving infused Parts instead of fear.

While writing this, I had an *aha!* moment and want to share it here. I want to call it a **Holy Instant**. In *A Course in Miracles*, the Holy Instant refers to one's choice to accept the energy of love over fear and unity over separation. This Holy Instant came to me the night before I was going to my hometown to see my mom, sister, niece, and grandniece. It is important to note here that in the days leading up to this Holy Instant, my sister and niece were experiencing conflict and stress, not least because of another significant development in my niece's life: she was pregnant again.

My Fixer/Martyr and Worrier Parts started to get a bit ruffled. It was not as bad as before I began the work of Illuminating, but there was enough of an emotional twinge that I was observing them very carefully. This Holy Instant happened, and it was the final layer left of the stories I held around my family and what I *thought* their expectations were of me. Here's how the Holy Instant unfolded in a yoga class:

My beloved yoga teacher, Michelle Gallant, led us in a chant: *OM GUM GANAPATAYE NAMAHA*. The meaning is a prayer to Ganesh to remove the obstacles that block the vision and manifestation of our unique gifts in the world.

As soon as the chant finished and we sat in silence, my Holy Instant occurred. At that moment, I realized that the time had come for me to stop judging my family as in need of any fixing, to stop putting pressure on me to fix, and to keep my world of inner peace and joy that I have worked so hard to achieve. In that instant, I felt more connected and unconditionally loving toward my family and myself. The pressure and fear were off. The love was on.

I came home skipping and told my husband. The following day, as I drove to my hometown, the Beatles song, *Across the Universe*, played in my head. The lyrics: *"Nothing's gonna change my world."* It was the most peace I had ever felt heading to be with family. And that weekend proved to be peaceful, too. When hooks came my way from people trying to hook into me energetically, I reminded myself that my family may live differently, but I do not have to judge. They may express their struggles, and I can show up and listen lovingly, offer observations, and even give advice if they ask for it—but I don't have to put pressure on myself to change or fix them. TRUE STORY!!!

My family is special, unique, sensitive, funny, kind, and fun when we remove the fear and anxiety. It's time to let go of the patterns and systems of the past that no longer serve me or them. It's time to appreciate my Parts and their Parts in new and positive ways, and that is actually happening more and more. I came across the following poem and felt it beautifully summarizes the epiphany I came to around not needing to judge my family, and realizing that I don't need to fix them.

A Medicine Woman's Prayer

I will not rescue you, for you are not powerless.
I will not fix you, for you are not broken.
I will not heal you, for I see you in your wholeness.
I will walk with you through the darkness as you remember your light.

Relationship with Friends

My relationship with friends has changed for the better in several ways. My Self-conscious, Perfectionist and Fixer Parts used to worry about being everything I could be to my friends. I would project stories onto them around the pressures I put on myself to be everything to them. Don't get me wrong—being a good friend, showing up for my friends, and offering presence, love, humor, and connection are among my highest values. What's different now is that it comes from a softer, less pressured place. Similar to my family relationships, I can separate what is *mine* and *theirs* more clearly. So, again, without the pressures that my Parts and their stories put on me, I can receive and embrace their love and connection without my convoluted stories making drama within myself for no good reason.

Another way my friendships are different is that the paranoid stories from my Self-Conscious Part can be managed more quickly. I used to worry for days that I said something wrong to upset a friend, or didn't do something for them and, therefore, must be a "bad friend." Thankfully, now, if that Part steps in, I will quickly remind that Part of all the ways I am a good, consistent friend.

My discernment of which of my friendships are balanced is also more apparent. I honor that information instead of overgiving or spreading myself thin because my Parts tell me stories that I need to go *above and beyond* to make sure a relationship is okay, even if that relationship may not be the healthiest or most balanced for me. And if it's not balanced for me, it's not for them. I also now have those tools to check out my stories with them, and let them know they can always check out their stories with me.

Lastly, I am more sensitive to the reasons for gossip. I often try to observe it compassionately, remembering it has more to do with the person gossiping as they try to sort something out. *Open, honest, healthy, and balanced.*

Dreams

When I say Dreams, I mean, *any healthy desire, goal, habit, behavior, or relationship we wish to have*. It can relate to our lifestyle, our career, our personal and creative expressions, anything we feel in our hearts that we want to actualize in our lives. I will write about this more in the next chapter when I talk about the *Divine Dream Dance*. You know it is a dream because it brings you joy and excitement when you imagine it.

Career Dreams

There have probably been many benefits to my career path since doing this work. The two rewards after doing this illuminating and transformational work that stand out are the way I show up for my clients now, and my job satisfaction.

How I show up for my clients now: Taking away the pressure of being the Fixer of my clients makes space for a much more calm and centered Part of me to show up in our sessions. Of course, I am there to assist them in solving their problems. But I am mindful that this is a *collaboration*, and if I am working more than the client, there is a good chance my Fixer Part is working overtime, which will not be helpful to anyone. I am so much more balanced and measured, so there is more ease in our work together. They receive more peace and clarity, and I do, too. Similar to the positive changes I have experienced with my relationships, without the pressure, I can be more myself, share more of my strengths, and show up differently. Even the pressure stories around needing to be highly productive are lighter. I focus on following my mission and sharing my gifts: following my heart, moving toward my North Star, and helping my clients do the same.

Job Satisfaction: I have gotten to a place where I can look back and see how everything was a stepping stone to where I am now. I can also look back and see when limiting stories kept me from truly going after what I longed to pursue career-wise: stories about money and security, and stories of not feeling good enough for my dreams. In my career, I am doing what my heart has *longed* to do. Psychotherapist. Author. Inspirational Influencer. Retreat Facilitator. PINCH ME! I'm living a dream.

This is what I wanted. The fact that I can now take everything from my journey and step into the role of being an Illuminator and help others know and live their dreams, too, is awe-inspiring. Providing space and opportunities for individuals, couples, and groups to heal, connect, create, express, and live a more full and free life is *beyond* my wildest dreams. I have arrived, and would not have arrived if I were living under any of those limiting stories around money, security, and worth. I wish this for everyone. We want to follow our passions and make work feel like PLAY! I know I'm not singing a musical on Broadway, but maybe I will incorporate that into my hobbies somehow. Today, I am okay with that. Everything I am doing and how I am doing it feels right within my soul.

Creative Outlets and Hobbies

We were born creative, and had to be creative and innovative to survive. Looking back at the everyday lives of our ancestors, it is evident that creativity was a vital and intricate part of every family and community—from nature to cooking, to making clothing, to quilt making, to building, to writing letters, to singing, to dancing, to gardening, and even hunting. There were so many more opportunities for connection and creativity. Now, our society is starving for creative expression. More and more, I am seeing and making these creative opportunities and expressions a reality for me. Writing this book is a creative expression that fills my soul so profoundly that I can't even describe it in words. I will discuss the various creative expressions, including music and singing, in the next chapter.

Journal Prompt: Can you think of a time when you bore the fruit of the inner work or healing journey you encountered? Describe it here and include details of the rewards you received.

CHAPTER 8

*

Obstacles When Illuminating *and* Transforming Our Stories

"Our deepest fear is not that we are inadequate. Our deepest fear is that we are powerful beyond measure. It is our light, not our darkness that most frightens us."
~ Marianne Williamson

Let us take a moment and name potential obstructions and obstacles when doing this work. Often, when we can name the challenges, we can disarm them. So, let us take a closer look at some reasons why we either give up or don't even start the work of illuminating and breaking through the stories between us and our dreams.

In this section, I offer many tools to navigate these challenges so you can maneuver yourself around the obstruction and not let it keep you from implementing the constructive and positive benefits of illuminating your stories. I have termed these tools "Shift Tips". These Shift Tips are quick and accessible ways to shift course and overcome obstacles on the way to your dreams. They help you navigate the discomfort of stepping into your dreams. Remember, everything we want is one step outside of our comfort zone. So, let's name the uncomfortable challenges right from the get-go, and you can refer back to this section whenever you need it.

While reading, if one or more of these challenges resonate, take the time to apply one of the Shift Tips so it doesn't invade the healing journey you have embarked on. You may also want to tag this chapter for future reference so you can use it whenever you find yourself hitting a bump in the road on your path to clarity and bliss. We can overcome these challenges together.

Obstacle #1

You Believe the Stories are Real or True

Do you remember when I described the experiment I wanted to do with my family at the beginning of this book? I wanted to check out the story I was carrying with them: the story that I needed to be perfect and fix everything, and if I didn't, well—then I was a failure. One of my brothers agreed to do it, and my other brother excused himself. When I asked that brother why he didn't want to be a part of it, he responded, ***"What if the stories you check out with us are true?"***

Good question, right?

If you can relate to this challenge or obstacle, consider applying one or all of these Shift Tips.

+ **Shift Tip: Very Little in Life is Black and White**
  Sometimes, there are elements of the stories that have truth. However, life is too complex, and the many layers of our lives and stories make things gray. Our stories often exist as an *absolute truth* in our subconscious and conscious. We make them into a cut-and-dry, black-and-white, conclusive, and absolute statement. You may recall from the section about my relationships and stories that when you illuminate the stories that are binding you, there are so many layers that they cannot be summed up in one unequivocal story, statement, or label. When you see things as black and white or all or nothing, it's often an indication of a false story.

+ **Shift Tip: Byron Katie and The Work**
  Ask yourself when thinking of the story: *"Is that true?"* In Byron Katie's book, *The Work*, she teaches how to approach our stories with discerning eyes and ask, *"Is that true? Beyond a shadow of a doubt, is that true?"* Notice your answer when you look closely at your story. My guess is you will find a sliver of it not being true. Try it.

+ **Shift Tip: Brené Brown's Hack**
  Whether at home, work, or with family and friends, examine the pestering stories swirling in your head by checking them out with others: *"The story*

I'm telling myself is…Is this story in my head true?" Remember, this is Brené Brown's spectacular "hack" that I mentioned in the chapter on Stories and Relationships, and it's so good that I'm saying it here again, too. I guarantee that it will ignite enlightening, healing, and powerful conversations regardless of whether or not the story is entirely off-base.

+ **Shift Tip: All of Me or Just a Piece of Me?**
If you find that a sliver of the story the person says is true, ask yourself: *"Do these stories define me as a whole? Or is this story just a Part of me?"* Maybe from there, you can identify which Part of you carries this story. Asking yourself this question will create more distance and containment of the story, and hopefully, you will see that this story is just a *piece* in the puzzle and not the whole puzzle. Once you know the specific Part, you can work to learn more about where that story is coming from and its intention and purpose. Is it trying to protect you? Is it a wounded or scared Part?

+ **Shift Tip: Gentle Investigation of the Story's Effectiveness**
Ask yourself these questions to further investigate the effectiveness of your story:
  - How is the story being used?
  - How is the story being applied?
  - How is the story working or not working for you?
  - How does the story define who you are or are not?
  - How does the story define how you react or respond or not?

Approach your investigation with a gentle curiosity. Avoid falling into the trap of interpreting a story as a generalized fact. Instead, strive for a balanced perspective that is constructive, helpful, and empowering, rather than destructive and binding.

OBSTACLE #2

General Resistance and Opposition

Another reason people hesitate to illuminate is resistance. Resistance is a term in therapy when a client is not receiving and implementing the therapeutic suggestions given by the therapist. We all come up against resistance whether we are in therapy or not. I hope that by mentioning it right away, you will be able to notice it, be aware of it, and keep reading this book and healing anyway, just like the quote from Susan Jeffers: *"Notice the fear and do it anyway."* Richard

Schwartz from Internal Family Systems also teaches us that, "Resistance is the way." In other words, when you face your Resistant Parts, make that your trailhead of investigation. Discover why the resistance is there, and the path to your dreams will open.

If you find the teachings of this book or work challenging, remember: *what we resist persists.*

Carve out 15 minutes of uninterrupted journal time to meet with your Resistant Part, and try this Shift Tip, which uses an abridged version of a tool from Internal Family Systems to help you get to know your Resistance Part better so that it isn't getting in the way of your constructive journey toward your dreams.

+ **Shift Tip: Getting to Know and Understand Your Resistant Part**
  1. Begin by connecting with your breath. Keep connecting with how your body feels on the inhale and how it feels on the exhale. Use any thoughts to bring you back to your breath; your only job right now is to connect with your breath.
  2. From this calm and neutral place, draw a picture of where you feel your Resistant Part in your body.
  3. Again, coming from this calm and neutral place, imagine the Resistant Part taking form outside your body; what does this Part look like? Draw it as best you can.
  4. Extend curiosity and compassion to your Resistant Part and ask what is its intention and purpose in trying to block you from illuminating and transforming your stories. Listen and write down how it responds.
  5. Next, ask this Part: what is your biggest fear if you move forward with illuminating and transforming the stories binding you? Listen and write down everything it shares. What is your Resistant Part afraid will happen by doing this work? Listen and write down everything it shares.
  6. Finally, thank this Part for all the wisdom it showed you. Acknowledge its desire to protect you. Explain to this Part your willingness to work through obstacles between you and your dreams. Express your hope that it will help you lead a more fully-expressed life, with healthier relationships and more feelings of joy and bliss. Share with this Part your request that you work together to help this Part soften so you can make these positive and constructive changes in your life.

Fears Your Resistant Part is Carrying

Below, I have listed fears that your Resistant Part may be holding. I have also included how I navigated my Resistant Parts in my dance toward my dreams. My real-life application and the Shift Tips I share here will help you find the courage to face these fears in your system.

Did your Resistant Part mention any of the following?

- Fear of an identity change
- Fear of being shunned
- Fear of the vulnerability of bringing something to light
- Fear of change and our addiction to the familiar
- Fear we will forget something and be foolish
- Fear that it is not a good time to illuminate

A navigation tip for this section is to go to the fear closely related to the message you received from your Resistant Part in the previous Shift Tip writing exercise. Or you can read through them and gather whatever nuggets you can. There are also Emergency Shift Tips at the end that you can refer back to whenever you bump into an obstacle.

Fear of an Identity Change

If your Resistant Part is carrying this fear, it may have told you in the last Shift Tip something along the lines of, *Who will I be without* _____ *story?* I know I was afraid that if I let go of the story that I need to be everything to my family and loved ones, I would lose my identity of being the "perfect sister/child/friend." Who am I without that story? We get so used to these stories or roles that they become a substantial part of us, and it's hard to trust that we will be okay if we let them go.

What helped me shift this fear was repeatedly realizing that the story no longer served me, served my life, and was no longer how I wanted to identify myself. In other words, I had grown out of the image I was so afraid of letting go of. What helped me shift was the acknowledgment that holding onto this old story and identity was getting in the way of what I wanted in this life.

+ Shift Tip: Rewrite the Negative Connotation

Another Shift Tip is to rewrite whatever negative connotation for the new identity you wish to step into. For example, when I first bumped into my fears about changing my story and potentially reinventing my identity, I feared the idea of seeming selfish. I had deep-rooted stories about seeming selfish and conceited if I focused on myself, went on stage, etc.

Thankfully, I have redefined "selfish," as our society has a negative connection to that word, especially for women. Now, I think of following my dreams as centered in Self (with a capital S) or aligning with my Authentic Self and moving from there. If you find yourself wrestling with the fear of an identity shift when you change your story, ensure you have a healthy perspective on how you define the reinvention.

+ Shift Tip: Holding Two Truths Simultaneously

One more Shift Tip for fear of identity change pertains to the gray areas and being able to hold two truths simultaneously. Once again, it's a handy tool for those who fear an identity shift by changing their stories. In my journey of rewriting the stories that my Fixer Part fiercely held on to, it was *not* about never being helpful or not being there for others anymore. I'm a psychotherapist, for goodness sake! I love helping people so much that I've chosen a profession where I do it daily. Everything I do is sprinkled with helpfulness to others. It is very much a part of me. The shift is the level of *extreme* that I attached to that role.

Now, the pressure of fixing or saving is lightened and comes with much less pressure and fear. Your Resistant Parts may be calmed by this shift, which means that our Parts will always be a part of our system. This work is about ensuring the Part isn't so extreme that it gets in the way of a healthy and happy life. Here are some examples of this Shift Tip in action:

- *"I have to fix everything for everyone, or else I'm a piece of crap"* shifted to: *"I take care of myself AND, from that place, help empower others to solve problems to the best of my ability."* OR *"I am a helpful person, AND I am mindful and measured to do it to the extent they are willing to receive my help."* *"I love being a source of support and offering creative solutions without the pressure of passing or failing, AND my identity and level of being liked and loved do not depend on it."*
- *"Putting others second to my needs is selfish"* has shifted to: *"I offer help from a healthy place with boundaries intact, and people receive the best part of me."*
- *"Without my Fixer in the lead, I'm no longer helpful."* This was shifted to: *"I will always have a helper and Fixer Part in my heart and in my DNA, and when it is regulated, it is healthiest for me and everyone involved."*

Fear of Being Shunned

There is also a big fear of being shunned due to changing our stories. What will people think if you are no longer in the story, the role, or the pattern you usually are in? I remember doing a deep-dive in coaching that showed the layers of my fear of not being enough for my family. I mentioned this earlier as well. Coach Kelly would guide me through the layers of reasoning I had around this story of needing to be everything for my family, and we would get to the bottom layers: fear my family would not love me and fear that I would be unlovable. I have shed this story and stepped into a different role, and my family still loves me—maybe even more so now. More importantly, I love myself more. *I love my life more.* I recently recorded a podcast with Coach Kelly (Episode #35), and she pointed out the power of me changing the story and the impact that has had because I am no longer projecting the story and fear that I will be shunned onto my family.

Similarly, I have noticed that my close and dear friends love me even more. They admire and support these changes. Even better, I believe my loved ones are getting more peaceful, clear, and confident Parts of me now that I am coming from a healthier and more authentic place rather than a place of fear (*People won't like me!*) and burnout.

That being said, there is a strong possibility that there **will** be people in your life who will struggle with your changes. Remember the clients who were upset with me in Chapter 4? It is possible that people may struggle with the change, and because they are attached to some of the extreme ways you were, they will struggle when that changes.

+ Shift Tip: What's More Important?

Here's a writing tool that I'm suggesting you use when navigating this fear:

1. Write down the new story. Write how this new story is healthy and constructive, and how it supports your North Star or goal.

2. Write down the people who have openly and consistently struggled with this new story and reinvented part of you.

3. One by one, make sure that it isn't just a story that they've shunned you. In other words, if they're still in your life in a positive or relatively neutral way and you *think* they don't like the new you, make a plan to check that story out with them like this: *"The story in my head is you don't like me because I am different, following my dreams, etc."* Then, let them confirm or deny that story. That will determine if it is accurate to have them on the list.

4. Once you have written down all of the people who are no longer aligned and have confirmed that is the case, ask yourself this question: *"Is it more important for me to follow my new story, OR should I resort back to my old way of operating to please the people who are struggling with the new me?"*

See where this writing exercise takes you. Are your Resistant Parts calmed by the information you gathered in this exercise? Does focusing on what is healthiest and best for you prove to be healthiest and best for everyone?

+ Shift Tip: Stay True to You
Remember to stay strong in your sense of self. Other people do not define you. So, even if you are being shunned or judged or you speculate that people do not like the new you, be true to you. Those meant to be in your life will follow and rise to the occasion; it is okay for those who don't. It's far better for you to be authentic and aligned with what feels true than pretend you are something different. Remember that other people have their own stories about themselves, and everything they do and say to you filters through them. Better to stay true to you.

+ Shift Tip: Will Following Your Dreams Impact Others?
Clients often share their fears that their partner won't love them if they change. I remember one saying that her husband may not love her if she loses weight. Another client said her wife would not support her going back to school for something she loves because it would take her away from being home. When I work with couples, I encourage them to share what they are passionate about and longing for with their partner and let them decide if that is not something they are willing to support. But you'll never know if you never ask or check it out with them.

There's a quote: "When your inner and outer worlds harmonize, your relationships do too." Following your dreams and breaking through limiting beliefs can be scary if it means losing the ones closest to you. Your connection will be stronger because you, your Parts, and your choices are more harmonious. At the very least, have the difficult conversation and wait to see if your partner feels black and white about you changing, or they may admit that it will be an adjustment and they'll be okay in the long run.

Fear of the Vulnerability of Bringing Something to Light

Another fear is simply in the illuminating. Essentially, someone is shedding light on a story that has been hidden or in the subconscious depths of themselves and the system (family, friends, etc.). To shed light on something hidden can be scary. It's the unknown. What will you find? Would it be safer if it remained hidden? Many people live in denial and delusion, and they are okay with it. You have to decide if you are okay living that way. I believe that continuing to ignore something or shove it away does not make it better. It comes out in odd ways, and the story will continue to be in the driver's seat of your life rather than you and your higher self being in charge. However, that is my opinion, and I have chosen a path to look inward at all of these things. You have to decide what kind of life you want to lead or what kind of story you want to lead your life. It is a conscious choice to look within and uncover obstacles you may have created that you don't even know they are there. If you want you and your higher self to lead your life, here are Shift Tools to help you find the courage to do so.

+ **Shift Tip: How is That Working for You?**
Many of us have heard the question Dr. Phil asks when his participants are in a destructive pattern or behavior that they resist changing: *How is that working for you?* How is living underneath a story that is causing you pain or distress? If you are just fine, it may mean you do not need to make the changes. However, if you want something different, and that behavior or pattern is *not* working for you, consider doing something different—like illuminating the story.

+ **Shift Tip: Awareness is 50% of the Solution**
Awareness has you halfway to a solution. And when we have that self-awareness, we are better in our relationships with ourselves and with each other when we are more self-aware. It is not only liberating but also empowering for everyone involved. The awareness and illumination will help drive you through the fear.

Fear of Change and Our Addiction to the Familiar

Many fear change because it's the unknown. "The devil you know is better than the devil you don't know" is often an expression my clients use when fearing a change of job, relationship, etc. Familiarity is safer than unfamiliar, which is likely the overarching story for our Resistant Parts.

When I try to empower my clients with Parts in the lead carrying this story, they will tell me: *I know my job, relationship, etc., isn't the healthiest and best for me, but at least I know it.* The unknown is never as bad as we imagine it, yet we will stay close to the familiar, fearing that edge of uncertainty.

We can be addicted to our stories. What do you think when you read that statement? I wonder if you thought, *"How could people be addicted to a story holding them back, a story that is in the way of realizing their dreams and experiencing joy?"*

It seems so bizarre that this would be the case, but we, as spiritual beings in this human world, struggle with that. Dr. Joe Dispenza takes this home for us in his book, *Breaking the Habit of Being Yourself*. His example is this:

A person comes home and finds their favorite pet dead. That event causes a strong emotional charge, naturally.

From that point, whenever that person sees an animal that looks like their pet, they are right back to that traumatic memory. Their whole body feels it.

Things shift so that the person doesn't even need to encounter something similar to bring them back. They randomly think about it and go back to that memory repeatedly.

This pattern eventually makes its way into their subconscious. Our subconscious is much bigger than our conscious. This emotional charge of the past begins to be familiar to them.

The adrenaline fight or flight feeling becomes the norm. Dr. Dispenza writes: *"We get addicted to our survival feelings—we love the rush from our troubles."* Then, your body responds as if the original traumatic event is happening now, not in the past. As a result, you are used to spending time in that state of grief, anxiety, and trauma and find your mind and body in that state, even if the present moment is pleasant and peaceful.

You almost look for ways to feel this. This can happen regarding stories that we think of that haven't even happened yet, but we imagine them as if they have. I often see this in clients who have had early childhood trauma or abuse and the response their body has ingrained from that experience becomes the norm. Relationships that are healthy become boring or foreign. The fight-or-flight is familiar. Fortunately, these habits can be reprogrammed. I encourage you to join me in breaking the addiction of stories that we interpret from our past and dreadful stories that we imagine regarding our future. Let's live from a more centered, peaceful and mindful place rather than from our traumatic, nervous-system-rattling stories.

+ Shift Tip: Joe Dispenza's "Rewiring the Brain"

Do you recognize that having a pattern like that can feel more like an addiction to *the familiar* than something helpful and reliable? For me, when I noticed I had a familiar pattern of feeling panic when my family reached out to me, I knew I wanted to make the conscious choice to avoid a trauma response or anxiety/panic as my familiar pattern. It started with being mindful of that. Joe Dispenza teaches these steps to help interrupt this addictive pattern:

1. **Awareness:** Be mindful and notice if you are addicted to a pattern that no longer serves you.

2. **Surrender:** Ask for help from something higher (God, Intelligence, Spirit, Source, whatever you believe). Surrender this pattern to your higher power and ask for assistance changing it.

3. **Dismantle:** When you notice it coming up repeatedly, say the word in your mind and heart: Change.

4. **Recognize and Rewire:** When you usually have a panic reaction, choose a different response and keep imagining yourself carrying out the new, preferred response.

This is similar to what I experienced when I did EMDR. I write more about EMDR in Chapter 11. It's a psychotherapeutic intervention that applies the brain science of reprocessing a memory. After those interventions, something that would normally trigger my former addictive response was interrupted. GLORIOUS!

Fear We Will Forget Something and Be Foolish

I see this come up a lot in couples counseling, especially around cheating and affairs. The person who feels betrayed feels it is vital to stay in the resentment, anger, or punishing parts of them to ensure the cheating never happens again. Sadly, this usually hurts the person and the relationship more and can keep them bound in stories that foster the cycle of cheating and general disconnection. It is like the saying, "Staying angry at someone is like holding a hot piece of coal and expecting the other person to get hurt." Often, stories that keep us bound in anger, unforgiveness, sadness, and unworthiness only keep us in an old story. It hurts us more than the other person and can cut us off from the goodness right before us.

In my own life, I have found forgiveness to be an incredibly liberating tool. I have learned to see forgiveness as a gift for me, my life, my relationships, and the other person. Forgiveness does not mean I will forget or be foolish. It just means that holding onto the pain or hurt no longer serves me. The true story is that we can forgive ourselves and others and remember the lessons we learned from the original pain and hurt. If you are caught in a cycle of pain and resentment and want to change, try these Shift Tools.

+ Shift Tip: Forgiveness Letters

Check out this newsletter I wrote in 2011 that shares my incredible journey in writing forgiveness letters. Not only do we experience physical health benefits when we forgive, but it is also the most powerful way to transform a story that no longer serves you. Before you panic and stop, know that you can always choose *not* to send the letter. Of all the letters I wrote during this experiment, I shared only two. However, I still felt the power of forgiveness with the unsent letters. I always recommend it to my clients and encourage them to read the letters to me. Read about this Shift Tip here, and if you feel inspired, try it yourself. I have had many clients equally moved when they implemented this way of doing a forgiveness exercise.

Title of the Newsletter: *I Forgive You. I Forgive Me. Written by Jennifer Carey 2011*

This past winter, I was feeling this underlying anger. I was on edge and irritable and could not pinpoint why. It was just below the surface at all times. At this time, I happened to come across many materials that talked about forgiveness. That's when I realized lack of forgiveness could be related to my irritability. When I started on this path, I immediately noticed that it was far easier to be grateful for things than to pay attention to the wrong someone else had done to me. As a result, it was easier to "ignore it, rationalize it, etc." This ease of denying is on top of the fact that anger is one of my least comfortable emotions. I also noticed that if I felt I had done something wrong, I wouldn't let myself forget it. How's that for a double standard?? We really can be hard on ourselves.

This Forgiveness Experiment started with a list. I decided to make a list of all the people I needed to forgive. And each day, I would write a letter to one of the people on the list. Maybe I'd send it, perhaps I wouldn't, but I would face it and GO THERE. That was the plan.

The List: Who do you think was the first person on that list? OH YES! I didn't even hesitate. I put ME. I was first on that list. I started with Dear Jennifer Helen Carey. I was serious and included my middle name to express that effect. Then, I just let the letter to myself flow from there. I wrote about the things I knew I needed to forgive myself for. Some of it had to do with not listening to myself or ways that I have hidden who I truly am instead of shining. I forgave myself for whatever came up to write. That was freeing. And as I mentioned before, the plan was to go to the next person on the list and write my letter to them the next day. It turned out that there was more than one day between these letters. So, I took my time and started feeling the layers peel away. Slowly, I noticed my relationships were improving, and I felt more at ease.

Lessons and Perceptions: As I moved through these letters, lessons started to emerge. I could begin to see what I learned from that particular person. Sometimes, I noticed the same pattern or lesson in two different people. I also started to see my role coming up and the various ways I still needed to forgive myself in those situations. Suddenly, another deep and powerful thing happened: I started to shift my perspective. As the letters flowed, I saw that I had more power than I realized, and there was something even better at work in these "misunderstandings." And like magic, I wasn't a victim anymore. For example, I wrote a letter To All of The Men I've Felt Hurt By, listing most of their names. As I wrote this letter, I saw it was much more about forgiving myself for doubting myself, my truth, my strength, and my capacity to feel loved and respected. I also started to see that, in most cases, I was grateful that they let me go and were sparing me the experience of being stuck in something that wasn't right for me. Then, I almost saw that in their "hurting me," they were actually "respecting me" because they didn't string me along. The forgiveness letter turned into a thank you letter that I didn't "end up" with any of them, and they honored me enough to call it quits, knowing they weren't the one for me. I learned a lot from reflecting on every situation in this light of forgiveness instead of a tone of defensiveness and resentment.

Relationships Improved: As I shared with people this experiment of writing forgiveness letters, they'd say, did you write one to me? I would respond honestly and mention what I learned in the process. My mother was one of them. She asked me to read it to her over the phone. So, I did. Tears flowed down my cheeks as I shared what hurt me the most: the fact that she struggles to accept who I have become. I wanted to know she was proud and didn't want to change a thing. She listened. She said she was sorry; I forgave her and can honestly say our relationship has improved. I also realized that accepting myself (not looking to her or anyone else for acceptance and validation) was more important. So, in forgiving her, I knew I needed to heal the relationship with myself. In the process of these letters, I saw that I took a lot personally, and there was a lot that I just needed to work on within myself. I'm telling all of you confidently that my relationship with myself and others improved after writing these letters.

Additional Benefits: In addition to improved relationships, I started feeling lighter, less angry, and less on edge. This gave me a deep perspective (vs. limited perspective) on all the situations I had felt so "wronged" by throughout my past. I was empowered by the lessons and strengthened by the experiences instead of feeling victimized, defensive, and deflated.

Furthermore, studies have shown that your overall health improves after forgiveness. In the article, Biology of Forgiveness, author MySahana cites research that proves everything from lower heart rates to improved oxygen and nutrient supply to your cells and tissues. WOW, Right?!

On that note, I suggest you do this experiment too. It all starts with a list.

One final thing: Here's a powerful excerpt from *The Four Things That Matter Most*, by Ira Byock, M.D.:

None of us need to wait to accept ourselves. We are worthy of self-acceptance and love right now. Even with our imperfections. We all have things we wish we hadn't done, even dark secrets that we hide shame. You may think other people don't have them, but they do. Yes, you are flawed, and you've made some mistakes. Who hasn't? It only proves that you are human. Please forgive yourself and show yourself love.

+ Shift Tip: The Part Afraid to Let Go of the Pain

Once again, the powerful tool of Parts Work steps in, guiding us to self-understand why a Part of us clings to the pain, hurt, and resentment that no longer serves us.

1. With a journal or with an IFS-informed/trained therapist, use the intense emotion of anger, sadness, or unworthiness as the trailhead.

2. Separate from that Part enough to have a conversation with it. In IFS, this is called *unblending*. In your mind's eye, imagine the Part takes a form outside of you and sits at a conversational distance from you.

3. Approach the Part with a sense of neutral curiosity. Ask about its intention or purpose in holding onto the anger, and write down whatever you hear in response. These parts often believe that holding onto the emotion helps them not forget and protects them from repeating the same mistake. Your Part may offer you even more wisdom, so listen and write down whatever you hear. After acknowledging and thanking the Part for wanting to protect you, with clarity and courage, sit with

it and explain to it (either writing or speaking out loud) that you will remember the lesson you need to remember from the hurtful situation. It is no longer serving you, your system, and your life to hold onto such strong emotions from the past. Assure the Part that when you need a reminder of the lesson, you can check in with this Part as a place of encouragement and support, not punishing or condemning.

4. Ask the Part to show you an image or object that you can carry as a reminder of setting free the pain/fear story, but carrying the valuable lesson underneath.

5. Thank the Part and yourself for the time you have given to this healing exercise and ask it to reintegrate with your system.

If you find this difficult to do on your own, ask a professional for support.

When Is it *Not* a Good Time to Illuminate?

Timing is everything. How do you know whether or not it is a good time to illuminate your stories and transform them? Here are a couple of Shift Tips to help you decide.

+ **Shift Tip: The 90-Day Rule**

Did you know that the *Diagnostic and Statistical Manual for Mental Health Disorders* advises clinicians to differentiate between Grief or Bereavement and the diagnosis of a Mental Disorder such as Major Depressive Disorder? When I was in graduate school, professors recommended waiting 90 days after a significant loss to make a clinical diagnosis.

When my father passed away suddenly in 2012, I felt the myriad of behavioral and mental symptoms that come with a significant loss. The lack of focus and difficulty concentrating; the rawness and sense that you could break out in tears or want to scream out of nowhere. And, magically, for me, after 90 days, something lifted. The grief was still there, but it was much lighter and not as severe.

The 90-Day Rule, as it applies to illuminating your stories, is this: if you have just gone through a significant trauma or major loss of any kind, *it is a time to be gentle with yourself* and allow your body to feel grounded again before doing the deep inner work of illuminating and transforming. Seek support and help that will enable you to process the loss or trauma gently. This work is a bit deeper and better if you have moved through the initial stages and shock of trauma or loss. You will know when you can focus, feel grounded, and are ready to dive deeper.

+ **Shift Tip: Watch the Shoulds**

When you say to yourself, "I should be illuminating," take a moment to do a gentle investigation: is this coming from your intuition and your gut? Is this from a place that knows it will be helpful, and are you in a good place/time and life to work on it? Or is it coming from a Guilt Part? An expectation from others? A pressure from something more destructive than constructive?

It can be tricky to discern. Using some of the wisdom from the 90-Day Rule, consider revisiting whether you are in a time and space in life where you can do this deep work, and if the answer is yes, keep investigating this work. However, if you feel like you are at capacity, maybe it's healthiest and best to put this down for 90 days and revisit it when you are in a more grounded place.

+ **Shift Tip: Avoidance is Not the Antidote**

Suppose you are facing a significant loss or crisis. In that case, the most important thing for you is to keep things simple and return to the basics: good rest, nutrition, restorative exercises, time in nature, and guided meditation—anything that will help restore your nervous system and get back to baseline.

This Shift Tip does **not** refer to those times. This Shift Tip is if you are in a stable and thriving place and are avoiding the journey of illumination and transformation of your stories because you do not want to commit. This Shift Tip is a gentle reminder that when we avoid looking at something begging for attention in our internal and external systems it doesn't just go away. As I mentioned in the section on nudges, what we resist persists. If you find yourself in a destructive state of avoidance of doing the work you know will help you achieve your dreams and desires, take the time to revisit the Shift Tips above and even the ones below to see if one can help you Shift into a more constructive place of aligning with your dreams.

+ **Shift Tip: The 51%-Versus-49% Rule**

There are various 51/49% rules out there. I will describe how the 51/49% Rule is helpful when you are hitting an obstacle on your healing and growth journey, and you know how important it is to you to make a positive change. This rule implies that you only need 51% of you to agree that taking the next positive step in illuminating and transforming a limiting story or belief. All you need is 2% more than the Part of you that is scared, resistant, and reluctant. Below is a step-by-step questionnaire to help you get to that

51% Part of being in the lead. I included examples of how I answered these questions when bumping up against obstacles within the parenthesis.

1. Write down the identity/role and the story you are afraid of losing.
   (For me, it was being everyone's Fixer/Savior/Martyr)
2. Now, write down all of the ways this identity serves you.
   (People love me; they look to me for guidance, and it's natural and enjoyable for me to be helpful.)
3. Now, write how this identity and story does NOT serve you.
   (I live for others first, often getting burnt out, working harder than the person who reached out for help, and sometimes helping them in ways they either do not want to change within themselves or enabling them not to have to change. I'm resentful when they do not seem grateful or appreciative for all I did for them.)
4. Next, write down your North Star/Desire: what dream silently pulls on your heart?
   (Being on stage, being an author, being a retreat facilitator, expanding how many people I can help/inspire.)
5. Write down what new identity or story is needed to help you achieve this dream.
   (It's okay to put myself and my dreams first.)
6. Next, write all of the benefits that will come from this reinvention or new identity.
   (I can share my message with more people. I will feel joy from being aligned with my dreams and following my heart; I can show up healthier and happier for my loved ones; I'm still helpful, just in a different way.)

Now that you have completed those steps, zoom out and take a moment to reflect on all of the information you have just gathered. Which is healthiest and best for you? Stay the same? Or move forward with illuminating and transforming to heal, learn, and grow?

If 51% of you wants to move toward your dreams and 49% is scared, take the power of that 2% lead, and take the next baby step. Follow that path. Use your passion and that 51% as the driving force.

+ **Shift Tip: Victim to Growth Mindset**

In Episode #32 of my podcast, I interview author and Transformational Coach JP Horgan, and he describes how he went from a mobile scooter to a marathon runner. He did not let the experts limit him with the diagnosis that he, "would never be normal again." I think it's a subtle yet fierce reminder that we can choose what kind of world we live in. Which world do you want to live in? Which story do you want to live your life under? We face this choice daily. Below, I describe a time my mom had to choose what kind of world she lived in, and I did my best to illuminate the friendliness of the situation.

My mom and I were at the ticket counter at the airport. She was returning to Florida, and I was dropping her off at an unfamiliar airport. Naturally, we arrived early, so my mom asked the ticket attendant, "How far into the airport will my daughter be able to stay with me?" He responded, "With the renovations, you won't be able to go further than the security, which is right there." He pointed up the escalator. Then, he secretly called us over to the side and whispered, "Here's a little tip so you and your mom can stay together. Ask for wheelchair assistance and express that you're going to wheel her to the door of the plane." And he even went a little further to say, "I know she may not need it, but that is how you can stay together longer." I thanked him and thought that was a kind gesture. He gave a warm smile and returned to the line of other passengers.

My mother, who is hard of hearing, asked for clarification about what he said. When I told her what he said, she was appalled at his suggestion that she needed the wheelchair. I explained at least three times that he was trying to be helpful. I pointed out how he gave us this tip in response to her asking how far we could stay together. He thought of a loophole that could keep us together and shared that with us.

She was attached to the story that he thought she was elderly and needy. I finally stopped and asked why she was choosing to see a friendly gesture as an attack. Why was it hostile to her when I saw it as kind and helpful?

I then asked her which story was more beneficial to choose. A few days later, she was still stuck on the story of being a victim. So, once again, I described how he intended to help us stay together as long as possible at the airport. I think she finally got it. You can see how different these mindsets are, and how we can choose to interpret an event. And that choice makes all the difference in how we look at the world.

+ Shift Tip: Listen to Illuminating the Stories that Bind Us Podcast Episodes

If you need inspiration to be courageous in facing these stories, listen to the participants of the podcast. Hear how this process transforms them and their relationships. Not only will their stories help you illuminate your own unique stories, but witnessing them voicing their stories will inspire you to share your own and help you trust the process.

Every participant on this podcast has shared a common thread: a positive shift in their lives when they voiced their limiting stories. By relating to and applying these stories to your own life, you're taking a significant step towards the life you truly desire.

+ Shift Tip: You Hold the Key

A very empowering concept to know and adopt is that *you hold the key*. Often, we depend on others to correct our stories and heal them so we can live a more peaceful and joyous life. We try to control how others respond to us, but ultimately, we hold the key that unlocks the power to change these stories and experience emotional freedom.

Think back to when I checked in with my brother to see if my "I'm not enough" story that I thought my family carried about me was accurate. Checking my story with him not only helped show how opposite it was to his feelings, but also how much it had to do with an internal struggle of my Parts that I was projecting onto my family. I held the key to healing the Parts carrying that story, continuing the work, and changing the day-to-day interpretation of events. Similarly, you can work to ensure that your stories are not being projected onto others, and that your Parts aren't working overtime out of fear or anxiety.

Conclusion

Remember that you hold the key. It is an inside job, and I am honored and joyous that you have called this book into your life to help guide you in transforming the stories that no longer serve you. I assure you this will be a positive and constructive change you will not regret. Your life is full and free when you illuminate your binding stories and break through all the limiting beliefs. You are empowered with so many more choices in your life because fear no longer drives the bus. On the other side, life is clear, and you can make decisions based on what is healthiest and best for you from a calm, confident, and courageous place.

Now that you have the tools to navigate the challenges that may come up in this process, it's time for you to begin the dance with your dreams, or what I call the *Divine Dream Dance*. It's time for us to transform the stories you have illuminated so you can live out your dreams.

Before we start dancing in the ocean of your dreams, I want to take a moment to pause, reflect, and regroup on what we have done to get here.

Pause, Reflect, Regroup

First, the part of this book you just finished took you on the Illumination journey. By reading my personal story and the stories of others, you believe in the power of becoming aware of the stories that bind and hold us back. In that process, you got clearer about a unique story in your life that may be keeping you stuck and holding you back. Remember, this is 50% of the solution.

Well, dear readers, the time has come for us to learn ways to transform and rewrite the story—the other 50% of the solution. Often, when I share the concept of illuminating the stories that bind us to people, they immediately want to know this second part. They ask with a sense of urgency: "Now that I know the story, *how do I get rid of it?*"

I like to use the words "dissolve" and "transform" when thinking of how we grow beyond our limiting stories. Like many things in life, the dissolving and transformation process takes time. It does not happen overnight. Often, therapeutic work is referred to as peeling back the layers of an onion. Every layer is useful and helpful and gets us closer to the core.

Think about it this way: You get to do the work around what you really and truly want in this life. You start to reprogram yourself to live from a place of pure desire that comes from within rather than outside of yourself. As you get clearer about what you truly want in this life, you shift from the limiting and blocking story you had to a place of authenticity and alignment.

It's time. Let's do this!

PART 2

Transforming the Stories

CHAPTER 9

✳

Defining Our Dreams *and* the Roadmap to Get There

"Miracles start to happen when you give as much energy to your dreams as you do to your fears."
~ Richard Wilkins

Where are we going and how do we get there?

As we transition from simply illuminating our stories to the roadmap of transforming them, let's begin at the destination: our dreams. I believe that getting clear on where you are heading (a.k.a your dreams), creates a compass you can always fall back on to give you a sense of direction. When you listen to your heart and what your soul wants to live out in this life, you'll have an easier time getting back on track when limiting stories and false beliefs jump out in front of you and try to take you off your path.

Before you take some time to focus on your dreams, let's get clear about the meaning of dreams as it relates to this book and process.

What is a Dream?

These are the words and phrases I'm thinking of when I talk about dreams:
- Goal
- North Star
- Desire

- Feels like a knocking on your heart
- Brings you joy
- Action oriented (exercise more, creative outlet, socialize)
- State of being (practicing present moment awareness, feeling more peace)
- Unique to the individual
- Often felt as a child before messaging from others and society sets in
- Uplifts your spirit at the very thought of it
- It lights you up

In his book, *The Big Leap*, Gay Hendricks talks about your Zone of Genius. This is another concept that aligns with the way I define "dreams". Hendricks describes the Zone of Genius as:
- The flow state: when you lose sense of time while doing a certain project or activity
- A deep sense of satisfaction and fulfillment while utilizing your natural abilities
- An intersection of your unique talents, passions, and strengths

Just writing this definition reminds me how much *writing* is a dream for me—it puts me in my flow state of joy and fulfillment where I lose all sense of time.

Journal Prompt: List and describe at least one activity where you feel the flow state and lose all sense of time.

Our Purpose and Our Dreams: Are They The Same?

Often, our dreams are also our Dharma, or our purpose in this life. Though it may not always be the case, what we are feeling knocking on our hearts is what we are supposed to be doing in this life. A book by Deepak Chopra, *The 7 Spiritual Laws of Success,* was significant on my spiritual journey. In it, Deepak Chopra says that everyone has a purpose in life or a unique gift/exceptional talent to give to others and become a service to humanity. The law of Dharma states that whatever that may be for you, *you will be successful at it.* It would be against the laws of the universe to not succeed at your Dharma. This realization brought me comfort and faith in the dance to my dreams.

I have felt some big dreams since I was a child (e.g., performing, becoming a psychotherapist) and some big dreams were born out of an epiphany or *aha!* moment that came later in life (like this book). I have felt that often, my dream and purpose intertwine. For example, spreading the word of *Illuminating the Stories that Bind Us* became a mission I felt in my heart after an aha! moment in private practice. There are other times when big dreams have come from that *aha!* moment, like this book or having a podcast. Now, there were, and are, plenty of little dreams born every day that are my steps toward the big dreams; like writing a newsletter or putting together a podcast team. Things like my personal therapy or process of illuminating the stories binding me or helping a friend illuminate something in the way of their dreams also qualify as little dreams.

Can Dreams and Dharma Change?

We also have dreams or knocks on our hearts that can evolve and change. What you felt strongly about at one time in your life may change and morph into something else for many different reasons.

Having biological children of my own is an example of this for me. (I could write another book about that decision, and I may someday.)It wasn't easy, especially because I had always pictured myself as a mother. I was one of those kids who played with dolls until I was 14. I would pretend to change their diapers and care for them in every way. It was in my DNA.

Then, a couple of things happened: I wanted a partner with whom I could learn and grow personally and spiritually. That became more important than finding a father for my unborn children. Before my husband and I became engaged, he said no to having more children. I went on at least a two-year journey to figure out this decision.

Ultimately, I did not want to lose the spiritual partner I had found in this lifetime and risk not living with him the rest of our days only to find someone who wanted to be a father. I realized I wanted to write this book, host retreats, and speak worldwide. And I knew that if I had children, I would invest all my energy into them. There was a severe mourning period and grieving period of not having children and having this dream come true.

Now I have come to a place of incredible peace. Fur babies and moving toward dreams like this book have been an enormous help. That is an example of our dreams morphing and changing and still being our dream and Dharma.

Here's a chart of Big and Little Dreams throughout my life. There are more, but these are the ones that stand out. I included dreams that did not happen because, let's keep it real, not every dream is meant to come true, and—there is still time left to achieve them.

Jen's Big Dreams	Jen's Little Dreams
• Become a Broadway musical actress • Become a teacher • Be a Mom • Go to college (Undergrad and Masters) • Travel • Become a psychotherapist • Facilitate retreats • Dance, sing, perform • Find a life partner to help me grow as a human • Spend time with family • Cook • Garden • Become an inspiring author and speaker • Find peace, enlightenment • Be a kind and helpful person	• Receive therapy • Write newsletters • Journal • Read self-help books • Create and run a private practice • Run a workshop • Run a retreat • Participate in retreats • Meditate • Take voice lessons • Hire a developmental editor • Practice yoga • Eat healthy • Practice self-love • Experience personal and spiritual growth

Jen's Dreams that Haven't Happened (Yet!)
• Become a Broadway musical actress • Be a biological mother • Own and/or run a retreat center • Share the power of mindfulness + performing arts in transforming our limiting beliefs and empowering us to live our best lives

What's the Difference Between a Big Dream and a Little Dream?

When I speak of a Big Dream in this book, I'm referring to the destination where all things come together in what you really and truly desire in this life. If you had a magic wand and could make your zone of genius a consistent reality, that's the big dream. It encompasses all the things described above. Big Dreams may feel too big or out of reach, but you know them by how much they light up your heart.

When I describe Little Dreams, I mean the action items, steps, and habits that bring you closer to the Big Dream. Little Dreams are the various stages on the journey toward your Big Dream. They often give you a taste of the big dream and can feel satisfying.

Now, let's put these terms into a real life example: Ever since you were a child, you have dreamt and seen yourself singing, performing, and speaking on stage. When you see others doing it, it lights you up, and you can see yourself there, too. The Little Dreams that were stepping stones to getting there were taking voice lessons, having karaoke parties, and receiving coaching and therapy to help you identify and transform the limiting beliefs, stories, and blocks you may have when stepping toward your dreams.

As we begin to use our Big Dreams and Little Dreams as guideposts on our journey to living our fully expressed life, the hope is that everything, big or little, lights you up. All of it turns you toward love and passion and though fear and limiting stories may trip you up, you never lose sight of what opens your heart to life.

You may remember in the beginning, I had you share a childhood dream. Whether it's the same dream you wrote in that first journal prompt of this book or a different one, I want you to get clearer on the calling on your heart.

Let's take a moment for you to bring a Big Dream to your mind.

Journal Prompt: What is your Big Dream? If you could do anything you wanted, with no obstacles and no stories getting in the way, what would it be? Some people get this answer by describing their perfect day. Please pause and take a moment right now and put your hand on your heart. What is it that when you imagine it, your heart expands? A sense of steadfast joy and excitement courses through your veins. It's a steady joy. A consistent excitement. Write down what your Big Dream is. Maybe it's the same dream you wrote down that you had as a child in the beginning of this book. Whether it's the same or different, write it down here and let your dreams be a North Star you keep in mind throughout this book.

Roadmap to Our Dreams

Dreams and our Dharma are closely related to a sense of joy and bliss. Writing about your dream and North Star most likely brought you a sense of contentment. Healthy relationships correlate directly with our dreams, Dharma, joy, and bliss. Why?

Firstly, we need people to believe in us and encourage us to achieve our dreams. It is human and social science. Secondly, the number-one correlation between people and happiness is the *quality of their relationships.* Sharing this Roadmap has become my mission because it will bring you closer to the connection and joy I describe here. I want everyone to feel this sense of contentment, joy, and bliss.

As we set ourselves up to learn about the path to our dreams, it is beneficial to highlight two things: One, it is not always easy, and two, believing in yourself and your dreams will be *necessary* to keep you on course. My amazing developmental editor, Mary Bergida DeLuca, shared an impactful story while reading this section.

She talked about a bishop who always knew he wanted to do mission work in Africa. Africa was the Big Dream that was knocking on his heart. However, every obstacle one could think of got in the way—illness, injury, and his trip kept getting put off. People would pity him and sadly say, "We're sorry you're not getting to do what you have dreamed." The bishop would respond, "I know it looks terrible, but I'm still on the path."

Sure enough, he achieved his dream and spent his final years in Africa, how he had always dreamed he would. When we stay on course and keep that North Star in mind, what is meant for you will not pass you by, as we observe in the story with the bishop.

In my journey toward following my dreams, my North Star, I have identified a nonlinear dance that is taken on the way there. This is the Roadmap I wish to share with all of you. I call it the *Divine Dream Dance* because there are twists and turns of joy, challenge, illumination, and breaking through stories, obstacles, fears, and doubt.

Before we dig deeper and learn this dance, here's a key to help you with the various terms in this section.

DIVINE: Something beyond the power of this earth drawing you toward it
Synonyms: *Higher Power, Higher Self, Universe Conspired, God-Inspired, All-Intelligence, Creator* (or whatever you associate with the Divine)
Examples: There are signs everywhere showing you that you are meant to do something. You get goosebumps and butterflies in your stomach when you think about it. You can *feel* it in your cells. You have unique and natural talents around it.

DREAM (awake): Something you know in your mind and heart that you would *love* to do. This can be as a profession, as a hobby, or as a bucket-list item. It can be something you have known you've wanted since you were born, or a desire born at a later time in your life.
Synonyms: *Imagination, North Star, Desire*
Examples: Something that lights you up when you think about doing it. You get excited when you think about it, and you have gifts and personality traits that go hand-in-hand with it.

DANCE: In this context, dance is the movement towards your dream. There are ups and downs, spins, slow moments and fast, small steps or big leaps, backwards and forwards—all moving you toward your North Star.
Synonyms: *Sequence, a combination of steps, Process*
Example: The six stages of following your dreams (which you'll find on the next page), from the knock on your heart to actualization and fulfillment.

PURPOSE (sense of): The thing you feel that you are meant to do in this life. Sometimes it is the same as your dream, but it doesn't have to be. It is possible to find a way to infuse this into every day, right now.
Synonyms: *Dharma, contribution to society*
Example: Sharing your gift of song and performance, helping others heal through performing arts

Now that we have your North Star defined and we are clear on the terms that we'll use, it's time for a Roadmap to help you get there: the Divine Dream Dance. Each of the following chapters is devoted to one of the six stages of this special dance toward our dreams. Here are the stages listed all at once, and then I'll go through them one-by-one.

Divine Dream Dance

Stage 1: The Consistent Knock on Your Heart
Stage 2: Bumping Against Your Stories
Stage 3: Asking for and Receiving Help
Stage 4: Little and Big Dreams Realized
Stage 5: Emotional Hangover
Stage 6: Complete Divine Flow

＊

The Divine Dream Dance

Stage 1: The Consistent Knock on Your Heart

"Let yourself be silently drawn by the strange pull of what you really love.
It will not lead you astray."
~ Rumi

A dream keeps knocking at your heart. There is something that you keep thinking about. When you think about it, it puts a smile on your face and you can feel it in your heart. Maybe you get opportunities to do some semblance of it. And when you do, you lose all sense of time. You are in your flow state. Something tells you that doing this will bring you joy, connection, and purpose, and you can't deny it. I have come to believe that this placement on your heart is connected to your divine. Whether you believe in a higher self or a higher creator outside of you, these dreams/dharmas that are gently knocking are what I believe to be a nudge on your soul toward your fullest expression.

For me, this is music and performance, writing, and speaking. When I am on stage, I come alive and feel so connected to everything and everyone. When I sing, the joy, and the expression of emotion fills my every cell. When I inspire through writing or speaking and sharing my stories in order to help others heal, learn, grow, connect, and create, I feel I am living my authentic and fullest expression of Self. I am in the flow. There is no time. Zone of Genius.

Visual Representation

An Arrow. This stage is represented by an arrow because you feel a silent pull toward what you love (and maybe the importance of having your whole body pointing toward it.)

Real-Life Example

I have already mentioned my dream of being a performer and how it regularly knocks on my heart. Something is pulling me to the stage. While working virtually with music coaches Mick and Tess, they suggested showcasing my music in a Songbirds Cabaret performance as a culmination of all the work we did with each other. As soon as they suggested it, I immediately buzzed: mind, body, and soul. I knew right away that I wanted to make it psychotherapeutic as well. Another dream that has continuously knocked on my heart since my 20s is becoming a self-help author and inspirational speaker.

When Mick and Tess planted the seed of performing these therapeutic songs, a collision of my Dharma and Dreams formed. I immediately knew how to emcee and organize the event: I would share stories and various ways to take the audience with me on a journey through those stories. I wanted it to be a healing, learning, and growth journey for everyone. A swarm of creative ideas for how I could weave everything together started swirling in my head. I planned to showcase this journey to teach and inspire others to follow their dreams, and I knew that in doing so, I was also allowing myself to live out a dream beyond anything I had imagined before.

The door of life answered the knock of these dreams and all of those knocks became a reality during a retreat-like festival that became known as The WOW STAGE. The WOW STAGE stands for: Weekend of Wonder Supporting Total Artistic Growth and Expression. This dream-come-true event occurred over the course of a weekend and brought participants on a journey of illuminating the stories that bind us and healing and transforming those stories through art, song, improvisation and performing arts. I mentioned two of the stories used in the cabaret earlier in the book. For example, I performed *Right to be Wrong* by Joss Stone to help me (and all of us) break through the limiting story that we all need to be perfect and not follow our dreams for fear of making a mistake. This Songbirds Cabaret was a dream come true for me. It pulled together everything: singing, performance, inspirational speaking, and a kickoff to a retreat. Pinch me! But it did not come without bumps and obstacles. Read on.

Arrow Representation: the Silent Pull

This was one of the many things that got me through the obstacles in stages 2-6. There was a soundless force pulling me in this direction that if it could be put into words it would say: "Follow this path for life" and "Follow this path for light." It felt like a mission, a purpose. My Dharma. This is what makes the *Divine Dream Dance* divine. These signs and this pull kept me going. I had dreams and various experiences that all corralled and pointed me toward the WOW STAGE. There were more than a few, but one that stands out was a dream of my deceased father pointing to a cave with flamenco dancers. And soon after that dream I was looking at a venue that became the first home for WOW STAGE, The Windhover in Rockport, MA and lo and behold, the director's mother danced Flamenco! Flamenco was sprinkled in books and paintings throughout the grounds. It was all coming together.

Journal Prompt: After reading about my silent pull, do you have a consistent knock on your heart or something silently pulling on you right now? Write your silent pull below.

CHAPTER 11

*

The Divine Dream Dance

STAGE 2: BUMPING AGAINST YOUR STORIES

"If you're trying to achieve, there will be roadblocks. I've had them; everybody has had them. But obstacles don't have to stop you. If you run into a wall, don't turn around and give up. Figure out how to climb it, go through it, or work around it."

~Michael Jordan

Those obstacles may come in the form of parts like: Self-Doubt Part, Imposter Part, Fear of Failure or Rejection Part. These Parts can creep in right now. This stage is completely normal and can almost be seen as a sign that you are moving toward your dreams. You can name the dream, as in Stage 1, and funnily enough that is when beliefs and stories start to rise. Stories and voices start to say things like:

- *"Do you really think you are capable of that?"*

- *"You can't support yourself and do that at the same time."*

- *"Who do you think you are, believing you could actually do what you want?"*

It's important that you take the time to listen to the Parts and their stories so that you can lessen their charge, shed and transform them. The more you get to know, identify and meet these stories with awareness and compassion, the better able you will be to navigate them so they do not hijack your path to your dreams.

Visual Representation

Snake. I have represented these stories as a snake for two reasons:

1. These stories will slide in and out of the other stages. I know often we hope that it's going to be a one and done type of thing. That it is linear and once you accomplish the first stage, you are finished and onto the next. However, in this *Divine Dream Dance*, there are layers. Furthermore, there is something about this dance that attracts our Fear/Doubt and Imposter Parts. The good news is that as you move through the process of illuminating and transforming your stories, the charge will dissolve and you will be able to move through the encounters with doubt and fear more quickly so that you will be able to take those steps forward.

2. A snake sheds its skin, which is essentially what you'll do with these stories and beliefs. Shed and shift what no longer serves you, layer by layer, leading your life authentically instead of from these limiting beliefs.

Real Life Example

My Parts started showing up full of stories to illuminate. All of my doubting, fearing, worried Parts, enter Stage Left. One by one, they started showing up terrified.

Self-Doubt Part: I bumped up against this one a ton, especially when it came to voice and singing. No matter how many lessons or practices, I still bumped up against the questions, *"Should I be doing this? Should I be singing? Maybe I should sing less? How is this a good idea? I sound awful and will make people cringe."*

Fear Parts: Fear of finances, fear of looking stupid, fear of not pleasing people, fear of… (fill in the blank). Whether it was my own created fear or the projected fear of others, this was another tough one. Call in *Illuminating the Stories that Bind Us* here! Every false belief you can think of was projected on a screen.

Imposter Part: *Am I a good enough leader/singer/facilitator to pull this off?*

People Pleaser: *Does my voice upset people? When I ask for help or ask for something, am I burdening and bothering people?*

Snake Representation

I wish I could say that these stories came up early on and then were healed by Stage 3 and never came up again. However, like the snake representing this stage, it slithered in and out throughout the stages all the way up until the night before I performed on stage in front of a live audience. Spoiler alert: the stories did not stop me. However, I needed to ask for and receive the help in Stage 3 in order for it to happen.

Journal Prompt: Is there a story that slithers in and out of your dream stages? Name that story and write it below so you can keep a gentle but close eye on it.

✳

The Divine Dream Dance

STAGE 3: ASKING FOR AND RECEIVING HELP

"Sometimes, all we need is just one person who believes in us and who will never give up on us. Someone who sees beyond our weaknesses, beyond our faults. Who knows that though we walk in darkness, we can still find our way into the light."

~Jocelyn Soriano

This stage is crucial. We often get caught up between Stages 1 and 2 and never reach this stage. If you are someone who knows your dream but can't seem to take the next step or make it past the next Little Dream, you can relate. Reading about making it through this stage is imperative. It takes a village, and we are wired to thrive in connection and community. Though part of the illuminating and transforming concepts and skills described in this book are here to empower you to meet with your stories and parts on your own, there are many times when we need assistance from the outside. My friends and family supported me, and there is nothing like someone who knows you well, sincerely telling you that this is what you were meant to be doing and that you can do it! It just takes *one* person to believe in you.

When I bumped into my stories, I called my therapists, a life coach, a shamanic healer, and a music coach. Sometimes we need people outside of our friend and family circle to be objective and share their gifts and expertise to help us through. They helped me face some of my stories that were in the way of my dreams. Stories like, *"It's selfish to want to be on stage and sing—give someone else center stage."* They encouraged me through the "am I good enough?" bumps. I have an incredible story for each and every person that I found. You can draw in the people you need to work through your stories—I firmly believe that when the student is ready, the teacher appears. When you know you need someone, state the intention of needing someone to help you and watch how the perfect person will appear in your life.

Not only do we need to ask for help—we also need to receive it. Make sure you do not have a story that could be blocking you from receiving help. Stories like, *"I don't want to burden anyone." "I can't afford to get help." "I'm not worthy of receiving support and love." "We are supposed to be independent."* You may have to do the work to dissolve these stories in order to receive help.

Here is a list of interventions and people you can call on to transform your stories and get through this stage. I am getting so excited for you just writing about these tools here because these are tried-and-true ways to help you throughout your journey of transforming the stories that are binding you. These tools will help you make interventions in your brain, create new neural pathways, and break the cycle of living underneath the same story day after day. These tips will help you make it through Stage 3.

I am proof of all of these tools working. The fact that you are holding this written and published book in your hands, or listening to it through your ear buds, is proof that I overcame stories and stepped into my Little and Big Dreams. These are the tools that helped me overcome the slithering snake of stories, shed them, and shift into a fully expressed authentic life.

Intervention Options

- **Mindfulness:** To me, this is at the foundation of everything. Present moment awareness. Noticing all of your thoughts with openness and curiosity and without judgment. Joe Dispenza guides us in a great mindful question: "What are you broadcasting every morning?" I have probably written it in this book already and here I am writing it again: Awareness is 50% of the solution. The more mindful you are, the more you are already making a difference.

- **Journaling:** Whether verbal or written, documenting your thought patterns and expressing yourself through words is incredibly powerful. When you can take your stories outside of yourself, you have much more access to your awareness of them and the changes you need to make.

- **Spiritual Practices:** Prayer, meditation, yoga, yoga nidra, faith, 12-step programs, surrendering to a higher power. Many spiritual practices and rituals will help in the way of transforming your story. A Course in Miracles is especially powerful in helping illuminate all of the illusions and stories we project onto ourselves and others.

- **Bibliotherapy:** The use of self-help books, like this one (*wink, wink*), can help you begin to see patterns and learn aspects of your own psyche you may have not been aware of before. This book could very well be one of the forces that you call in! Remember, you can also refer back to the Shift Tips you learned in the previous chapter for wisdom and guidance through this stage.

- **Psychotherapy:** Any type of therapy is going to help you discover the story and voice it—which is powerful in and of itself. Furthermore, if we can not only voice it but also be witnessed from a supportive energy/entity, etc. the transformation is exponential.

  » *Creative and Expressive Arts Therapy:* These therapeutic approaches, including art, music, drama, dance/movement, poetry, and play, are rooted in the arts and theories of creativity.

  » *Performing Arts Therapy:* This is not a noted form of therapy—yet. (Remember that is one of my Big Dreams!) I believe that when our creative and artistic expressions are witnessed in a safe and supportive environment, we increase the power and effectiveness of transforming our stories.

  » *Narrative Therapy:* By breaking down and rewriting the problematic and demonstrative storylines or narratives in our lives, we are empowered to become the author and separate ourselves from our problems.

  » *Internal Family Systems:* IFS identifies and addresses multiple subpersonalities or families within our mental system. They can be wounded parts like guilt and shame, or managers like perfectionism and control. These Parts can often work to an extreme and carry stories that become obstacles to our dreams. Our Parts *think* they are being helpful. By looking more closely at the dynamics and conflicts within ourselves, we can understand our inner world. This helps create a more balanced, harmonious, smoother path to our dreams.

» *Laughter:* The use of laughter can help improve physical and mental health and overall well-being. It uses humor to manage stress, anxiety, anger and problem solving. Laughter has a way of illuminating difficult truths while easing tension at the same time.

- **Life Coach:** I have already mentioned, Kelly Russell, the coach I work with. She actually coaches from A Course in Miracles, and she is a licensed psychotherapist full of tools to help transform your stories. Kelly and I dove deep to see what stories lay beneath whatever was disturbing my peace and keeping me stuck. Coaches have an incredible way of helping you find the gap between *where you are* and *where you want to be.* They help identify the obstacles getting in the way of your fully-expressed life. There are different types of Life Coaches, so you will want to make sure that you choose one that aligns with what you need in order to accomplish your goals and dreams. First, get clear about the step you need help with. If it's a general need for personal development and getting unstuck, then you may choose someone who is a Transformational Life Coach or an Accountability Coach, or a Self Discovery Coach. If your dream has to do with a creative expression, you may choose a coach that specializes in that art, voice, music, writing, painting, etc. And if you are looking to achieve a dream in leadership, you may choose an Executive or Business Coach. There are also Professional Development Coaches. Get clear on what you need and I trust you will find your person/people.

- **Shamanic Healing:** Oftentimes our stories come from a trauma that we experienced in this life. And for those that believe in past lives, it is possible that a story is carried over from a past life. In Internal Family Systems therapy, Dr. Richard Schwartz teaches us about *legacy wounds,* or stories that come from our ancestors. Did you know that they can actually find our ancestral trauma in our cells and DNA? And sometimes talk therapy cannot seem to touch these stories. Shamanic healing helps touch and transform those things that lie in our subconscious and DNA. As I mentioned earlier when I spoke of my dark morning of the soul, shamanic healing pulled me through that. When I started using shamanic healing to heal my stories, I was brought to higher levels of understanding what stories I needed to transform. I also received clarity on the stories I wanted to step into. I worked with Lisa Desrosiers—her contact information is also in the back of this book.

- **Hypnotherapy and EMDR:** I could write a whole book on hypnotherapy and its benefits. In a relaxed state with some awareness, we can bypass some of our blocks to healing. I have experienced both hypnotherapy and EMDR (Eye Movement Desensitization Reprocessing) and the impact on my life, my stories, and my past trauma has been gentle, subtle, and profound. EMDR has been recognized for its impact on Post Traumatic Stress Disorder. Memories that previously made me shudder or that could seize and bind me, have little, if any, impact on me anymore. (Another shout out to Kelly Russell, as she was the one who performed EMDR for some of my childhood/young adult experiences that fed the story of needing to make everything okay for everyone.)

- *Illuminating the Stories that Bind Us* **Podcast:** This is an excellent way for you to begin breaking through the story binding you. Just the act of sharing it and then hearing it back is powerful. I always create an anonymous, safe, and compassionate space for you to feel comfortable and be witnessed. What is beautiful about that option is you get the opportunity to help others who can relate to your story. When you illuminate your own story, you help shine light on theirs as well. Paying it forward; a gift that keeps giving.

If you can, I recommend incorporating at least a few of these into your life in some way to help you break through a story that is binding you. It may seem overwhelming but if you take it piece by piece, you will find the journey quite effective and powerful.

I have used every single one of these interventions and my personal stories around how and when I used them are peppered throughout this book. Don't be afraid to reach out and ask and receive help. It is beyond worth it.

Visual Representation

Heart, helping hands and key/lock. The heart represents your dreams. The helping hands signifies our need to be for asking and receiving guidance and help. The Key in the hand signifies how you hold the key that opens the gates to giving and receiving this help.

Real-Life Examples

I can say with 100% clarity and confidence that if I did not ask for and receive the help from others, realizing my dreams through the WOW weekend in

Stage 4 and the rest of the stages, would not have happened. Here's all of the ways I used the tools that I described above.

- **Mindfulness:** Daily meditation and just staying aware of my thoughts and stories helped me stay one step ahead. There are Internal Family Systems meditations that helped me meet with the Parts that were freaking out and help them calm down. Sometimes my therapist would facilitate the process of me meeting with my Parts that were sharing stories of fear, or I would just listen to recorded meditations on my own. Focusing on present moments in nature was also a recharge for me.

- **Journaling:** To get all of my Parts and their stories and their feelings out on paper is so helpful in many ways. Again, these could be journal prompts from my therapist or coach or just free writing and getting everything out.

- **Spiritual Practices:** Yoga really helped me get into my body and out of my head. It's the one time I could be unplugged and have nowhere to go and nowhere to be other than with myself. Spirituality is so big for me. I am communicating with what I believe to be Source, Spirit, a higher power all day long. Sometimes I speak directly to ancestors, asking my father for help and guidance. I literally believe in the quote by Wayne Dyer: "We are spiritual beings in a human world," so it is hard to separate this resource from every thread of my being. Furthermore, the idea that this work is my Dharma helps me conquer the Doubt and other Parts because living out my soul's purpose is top priority for me.

- **Bibliotherapy:** Reading self-help and metaphysical and spiritual books really empowers me. The biggest books of inspiration that helped me through these stages at this time were: The Big Leap by Gay Hendricks and Daring Greatly by Brene Brown. I also watched the movie by Wayne Dyer, called The Shift, just before the big weekend to give me some steam and a reminder (*this would be better referred to as Cinema Therapy).

- **Psychotherapy:** I was seeing an Internal Family Systems therapist during this time. She helped me with accessing my Self and my courage and confidence. She also helped me with balancing my Parts when leading The WOW STAGE team.

- **Life Coach:** It was actually my Life Coach, Kelly Russell that led me to the book The Big Leap. Her steadfast support and believing in me, helping me confront limiting beliefs and Rock My Joy (her tagline), serves as the wind beneath my wings. And let's not forget Mick and Tess, my music coaches. They were the force behind all of this. I also hired a virtual voice coach, Christa Pfeiffer, to help me too.

- **Shamanic Healing:** There is something about Shamanic Healing that reaches a wisdom that just cannot be accessed by regular psychotherapy or coaching. When I worked with Shamanic Healer Lisa Desrosiers, I saw vivid images that carried profound and uplifting messages. Those images and messages helped me rewrite the stories that would have blocked me from moving toward my dreams. I also had a lot of images of being on stage during our healing journeys together.

- *Illuminating the Stories that Bind Us* **Podcast:** Doing this podcast is such an inspiration to me. I get energy and motivation from the courageous participants and insightful guests. It just fuels me to keep being the change I wish to see by breaking through my own false narratives and limiting beliefs.

Friends and Family

I have acknowledged my friends and family throughout this book. Their belief in me and their support, encouragement, and enthusiasm were necessary and absolutely priceless. We need a tribe. My friend Kelly Cherry stepped up to be the guitarist with me for this weekend, and I don't think I could have done it without her.

The WOW STAGE Team

They kept things moving and were there when I felt like I could easily give up. We need a tribe, people!

Here's a more specific real-life example of how Stage 2 really tripped me up, but I was able to call on friends and family, and flex my spiritual muscles just before I experienced the euphoria of Stage 4.

How I Received Help and Not Going at this Alone Carried Me Through

I call this the "low before the high" of that original WOW STAGE. After all, life is a series of ups and downs, correct? Thankfully, I got through. Even though I wanted to bolt, the people around me kept me going.

My "low before the high" came during dress rehearsal. It was the night before the WOW Stage's Songbirds Cabaret. Our team had arrived from Florida and California, and it was time to check out the stage. I remember being exhausted and enthusiastic all at once. It was time to put more than a year of practicing singing with Mick and Tess, my voice coach, and Kelly, my guitarist, into action. It was time for a retreat and festival weekend.

It was then that my worst nightmare began. I started to sing, and I looked out at my team watching and saw the gestures and facial expressions. I heard the comments, and I heard their suggestions of how I needed to warm up and how I sounded tired. I quickly revisited the story in my head: *"I sound awful! This was a bad idea!"*

In exactly 24 hours, I would be singing on stage in front of an audience, and based on my interpretation of the reaction during dress rehearsal, the story resounding in my mind was, *"I sound awful."* Talk about the fall of innocence—I assumed I would sound wonderful and everyone would pick up on the magic of the process immediately. Maybe we were all tired and trying to transition. Horrified, I turned to the guitarist, my dear friend Kelly, and hugged her and just cried. I squeezed and hugged her as tears streamed down my face. I completely imploded. I was spending the night at the venue, so my husband left to head home. I remember longing to go home with him. To be safe and sound in our bed. I wanted to run away from this and not look back. The *flight, flight, freeze* was fully ignited. The shame and embarrassment response of isolation was also ignited.

This is an important reminder for these stages: we are tested right before we accomplish our big dream, and we will want to give up *just* before. Please do not be fooled by that slick slither of the snake. Just shed the stories, notice the fear, connect with the knock on your heart, and do it anyway! Remember the Michael Jordan quote in the previous section: find a way to get through the obstacle.

Our decision to postpone the rehearsal until the next day was not an easy one. The day had been long, and the strain was evident in my voice. The disorientation of performing on stage, a feeling unfamiliar to those of us who primarily practice offstage, added to the challenge.

I cried myself to sleep. I woke up at 5 am and knew the only way was forward and through it. The Songbirds Cabaret was happening. People bought tickets. People registered for this incredible healing weekend. Our team and other performers were all planning to be there. I kept moving forward.

Dayna Wood, a dear friend and colleague, happened to be there as a participant, and we shared a cabin located close to the stage. We could hear the hustle and bustle of preparation and practice. It was time for me to face the music again. Dayna and I sat and talked about "the why."

Why was I doing this? I shared with Dayna how vital the mission of The Songbirds Cabaret was to me. It had evolved to be so much more than a culmination of the work I did with my music coaches, Mick and Tess. I wanted a parallel process to occur. I wanted to take the audience on a journey *alongside* me. While they are witnessing me facing my dreams in one of the most vulnerable ways possible—singing—I would inspire them to follow their dreams and overcome the stories blocking them. This unique cabaret was about connection, illuminating the stories that bind us, and using creative and performing arts to break through those binding stories.

On our beds in our cabin, Dayna and I meditated on the mission. It is so important to me to be a channel of Divine inspiration. We imagined THE MESSAGE coming through at The Songbirds Cabaret, not the nightmare I had chosen to take from the dress rehearsal experience. Our fantastic team helped me make this mission a reality. As soon as I locked in on that mission, my Dharma, and remembered our team, I felt clear. I caught the wave and surfed it for a long while. I connected to the mission and dreams that have been knocking on my heart, and rose to the incredible occasion we had created. I danced with that wave to Stage 4.

Heart, Helping Hands, and Key/Lock Representation

My Shamanic Healer Lisa Desrosiers often reminded me that I showed up and allowed myself to receive her help, and that takes courage and vulnerability. It's true—I had to bravely open the gate to allow myself to ask for and receive help and guidance throughout this stage.

Journal Prompt: Write one of your dreams below. Then, write who you will ask for help in making your dream a reality. Next, write how you will receive that help (e.g. showing up, committing). And lastly, write a declaration that expresses your openness to asking for and receiving help.

*

The Divine Dream Dance

STAGE 4: LITTLE AND BIG DREAMS REALIZED

"All of our dreams can come true."

~Walt Disney

You step into your little dreams and big dreams. You are living the desires of your heart. The dream is realized and you are in a complete flow state of bliss and joy. This is your zone of genius. It is euphoric. Your schedule is full of the things that make your heart content. You feel authentically connected to yourself, your desires and for many of you, your purpose too!

Other characteristics of this stage include feeling empowered, full and free. You are carrying a sense of clarity and trust for what you feel in your heart and your calling. Your mental health is also generally positive and constructive because of the joy, satisfaction and peace you are experiencing while following your heart. You feel free and full.

Visual Representation

A stage light beaming down on a stage. Whether your dream is to perform or not, this signifies the light shining on the unique dream that only YOU can do because you are the only one that can be you.

Real Life Example

Here is the setting: It's an hour before The Songbirds Cabaret. I stand firm and centered on the mission as I described above. Shannon Ward and I are practicing voice drills in the cabin next door. Shannon would be debuting her song, "Lucky Me". We feel great and excited. I felt firmly grounded and clear, ready to be the speaker and singer for this debut cabaret.

I explained to the audience that they would be on a journey alongside me toward my dreams of singing and performing. I invited everyone to think about a dream that they had had since they were children, and that perhaps there were stories that kept them from following those dreams and desires.

When I introduced my songs, I explained what story I was intending to break through, and the song that Mick and Tess Pulver prescribed to help me do so. For example, the first song was "Right to Be Wrong" by Joss Stone. This song aims to break through my perfectionist tendencies and fears that I would never be enough for my family.

My dear friend Kelly Cherry accompanied me on acoustic guitar. I took a deep breath, and as the first line came out of my mouth, I heard it entirely off-key which was something that happened often with this particular opening when I practiced it with my beloved voice coach, Christa Pfeiffer. And when I heard it off-key, I just giggled inside and kept going. I had fun. I felt the song with my whole being and mainly felt on key for the rest of the song. I broke through the need to be perfect by making a mistake as soon as the show started. I continued through other prescribed songs, ending with "Feeling Good" by Nina Simone, a song to remind us to find the simple things to help us feel good after two and a half years of the grueling global pandemic that precipitated this event.

While I sang and spoke, I saw tears on people's faces. I lost a sense of time and was mesmerized by the co-healing, learning, and growing. I was in my Zone of Genius, as Gay Hendricks would call it—that flow state. I felt everything I described under the definition of your dream state: completely aligned with my Dharma and the desires I have felt knocking on my heart. Imagine if I had given up. Imagine if I never made it to this beautiful summit. The dream was everything I had hoped it to be *and more*.

During intermission, people approached me, hugged me, and told me how inspired they were. It made them want to follow their dreams, sing, and participate in this retreat weekend. Some said they could feel themselves healing and growing. Afterward, the comments included:

"I was meant to be here, this was so inspiring"

"That was a year's worth of therapy in one night"
"You were so brave and courageous."
"You are a powerhouse!"
"I want to do this and commit to everything—when are you having it again?"
"I feel so much joy—this was so uplifting."
"I could relate to everything you said."
"You are a rockstar!"
"You have such a strong stage presence."
"You are so articulate, and an amazing storyteller".

Knowing that people felt all of those things and knowing how I felt—completely in my zone of genius, completely in my flow—left me with a complete, natural high. I had a smile on my face, a contented heart, and an energized body. I went to sleep that night feeling much different than the night before. I remember hugging my assistant Cassidy Brooks-Bowling and just looking in her eyes and saying, "We did it!"

I wish I could leave it there, folks. And there will be many times in the future I can skip this next stage, but not this time. A couple of days after I achieved my Big Dream of the WOW STAGE, I crashed. I crashed hard.

And I questioned everything.

The silver lining to this crash is that what I experienced next helped me experience firsthand what can happen to us right after we achieve our big dreams, so I can write about it in this book and help us with the next stage. What I share about the next stage will prepare you to keep going after you achieve your dreams.

The sky's the limit when you are in your flow—but I had one more low to make it through.

Light Representation

Well, the light shining down on a stage could not be more appropriate than my example. That was literally the scene of me on stage, light shining down, at the microphone, singing, speaking and healing. My Dharma.

Journal Prompt: Describe a moment in your life when the dream that you wrote in Stage 1 is fully realized, as if that realization of that dream has already happened.

✳

The Divine Dream Dance

STAGE 5: EMOTIONAL HANGOVER

Or, as Brené Brown calls it: Vulnerability Hangover

"Vulnerability is the path and courage is the light."

~Brené Brown

Doubt. Pit of despair. You feel raw. You are questioning everything. This is a tough stage. Inner and Outer Critic Parts will step in during this stage and the stories they carry are louder than they were in Stage 2 because your dream happened and it's out in the world.

You have started to SHINE, and you are sharing all these incredible yet vulnerable parts of yourself. It feels raw because this is at the *core* of your being. Your dreams are like your babies that you just birthed outside of yourself. What will people think of your authentic expression? And what will some of your protective parts do when they know it's really happening? You are really and truly doing it.

Self-Sabotage Parts or other Fire Fighter Parts may begin hijacking your system to numb your intense discomfort during this stage with food, alcohol, or drugs to avoid intense feelings during this stage. I highly recommend Brené Brown's book, *Daring Greatly*. She helps you get beyond the inner and outer critics and live a life in the arena you are meant to live and shine in.

You must also call on your reinforcements again, like you did in Stage 3. You may want to give up on your dreams, and we don't want that to happen.

Visual Representation

Child's pose. This image represents the innocence, surrender, and trust that need to happen in this stage. Go into a child's pose. Remind yourself that there is a reason you are being pulled toward your dreams. You will be back to the bliss and endorphins of Stage 4 in no time. One day at a time. One little dream at a time. Keep going.

Real Life Example

This stage did not start until late Sunday or early Monday after the WOW STAGE weekend. To reacquaint you with this storyline: the Songbirds Cabaret was Friday. We had workshops on Saturday and Sunday that were absolutely amazing. Everyone left with a smile and a feeling of love, belonging, and growth. I was still riding high. It was such intrinsic satisfaction, even if I was a little exhausted.

Then, it started happening. My mind and all the Parts and their stories took hold. I started repeatedly playing the compliments that people shared with me in my head (the ones I wrote under Stage 4).

However, instead of feeling those compliments so purely as I did when I first received them, I started thumbing through them in my mental filing cabinet, looking for any compliments about my voice. The guitarist (Kelly Cherry), my husband, and my cousins had mentioned my voice. And my niece said, "You crushed it!"

But suddenly, the handful of people who shared their feedback had nothing on the two handfuls who said amazing things but didn't mention my voice. So, my brain went to the worst possible aspect of an extraordinary weekend, and a story was created: "I sounded awful!" I sang in front of a bunch of people, and it sounded awful. To say that my skin started to crawl is an understatement.

I panicked and looked for available footage to confirm this story. I listened to one glimpse, heard my voice off-key, and stopped watching. I started to think of specific people in the audience and thought, "Oh no! Did they cringe? Please, God, please say people did not cringe. How can I live with myself if I made people cringe?" I started to go into some shameful responses of wanting to run and hide or argue with people, saying that this was not about having the perfect voice. I wanted to remind all of the critics I was creating in my head that this weekend's mission was about following your dreams and working through the stories we make that keep us from achieving them, not a Carnegie Hall performance.

I had imagined (*imagined*—this is all a cage I was creating in my head) all of these noses up in the air at me when, in reality, there were only two cases where someone spoke explicitly to my voice. One person said, "I was worried you were going to feel embarrassed." (Yes, that was an ouch), and the other said, "Definitely practice more—you can tell it makes you happy! Just keep practicing." Again, not so bad, but my head took it to places I cannot even tell you. Even after I had actualized the dream, the slithery snake had made its way.

So, we are back at calling on all the reserves (a.k.a Stage 3) in order to not let these stories sabotage me.

First, Bibliotherapy helped me. I mentioned earlier how Brené Brown's book, *Daring Greatly,* was monumental in helping me through this stage. This quote by Theodore Roosevelt was made familiar to me through that book and helped me stand stronger:

> "It is not the critic who counts: not the man who points out how the strong man stumbles or where the doer of deeds could have done better. The credit belongs to the man who is actually in the arena, whose face is marred by dust and sweat and blood, who strives valiantly, who errs and comes up short again and again, because there is no effort without error or shortcoming, but who knows the great enthusiasms, the great devotions, who spends himself in a worthy cause; who, at the best, knows, in the end, the triumph of high achievement, and who, at the worst, if he fails, at least he fails while daring greatly, so that his place shall never be with those cold and timid souls who knew neither victory nor defeat."

Second, I shared with my therapist how unbelievably vulnerable I felt—the rawness, the crawling out of my skin, the wanting to run, to numb this feeling. And I will never forget her saying, "This must be why famous musicians overdose." I was like, YESSSSSSSS! This is such an intense feeling. And it is so complicated because I'm feeling so embarrassed about something that felt so good at the time. So right. So perfect.

Third, I had a follow up session with Mick and Tess Pulver, the coaches that planted and nourished the seed of this WOW STAGE journey. I literally sobbed the whole time, expressing my fear that people in the audience cringed. I tried so hard to make peace with the fact that this was about the mission, and so many people expressed how amazing it was. So why am I feeling such a strong fear?

Then, it was time to implement the surrender and child pose. To turn this over to something higher. To hold the questions while letting go of the stories and no longer feeding them. I was left with the question in my mind and in my heart: What do I do with this crash? How do I use it to inform me moving forward? Does this crash mean I never follow my dreams again? Does this crash mean I just write and speak at The WOW STAGE—no more singing? Does this crash mean that I encourage other people to do it because I know it will bring them joy, connection, and help them transform their dreams but I will never do it again? Do as I say, not as I do?

I kept these questions. I held them. Meditated on them. Continued to bring them to therapy, etc. I sat with the uncomfortable and the raw. I even drummed up the courage to watch myself sing from start to finish.

A year and a half after I performed at the Songbirds Cabaret, I happened to be in the room with two people that I had thought had their noses up in the air. They came up to me and said, "You are such an amazing singer. I still remember how you made me feel that night."

See? I had projected so many stories onto them.

More Wisdom for This Vital Stage

It's easy to fall into the "give up" trap. But remember—it's always darkest before dawn. This darkness, I believe, is a catalyst for personal growth and success. It's a necessary part of our journey, illuminating the path to our next stage of bliss and joy. So stay the course, hold onto your belief in yourself, and keep pushing forward!

The most important thing to do when this stage of the dance comes up is *surrender*. That may seem counterintuitive to the idea of not giving up. Let me explain.

It's almost like a moment of disassociation. You will cave if you listen to all the Inner and Outer Critic Parts. Therefore, you need to listen to, then kindly ignore, the sabotaging voices. Remember, you already allowed them to share what your Parts needed to process in Stage 3.

Here's another way to explain it. I had the incredible honor of witnessing the birth of my best friend, Melissa Gannon's firstborn. I watched my best friend get into the most astonishing zone where it was just her, *giving birth*. No distractions, no attention to anything else. She wholly surrendered to her body's wisdom and intelligence and leaned into the birth doulas to push this baby out. Despite the pain, despite the various people in the room, at that moment, it was just her and the birthing process.

THAT. That is what is needed. When I have the moments of extreme vulnerability classic of this stage, they'll often come out of nowhere. I will have a flash of a dream I just completed (sharing a part of my book with someone) or a dream to come (booking a venue for a retreat). I'm excited one minute and the next, terrified. What gets me through these moments of doubt is this sweet surrender to the silent pull I described in Stage 1. I get into that focus of giving birth. And I focus on the dream/desire/North Star, and I say, "Okay, Divine Dream, I'm following your call. I'm not giving up."

That is the focus. I am surrendering to the pull. I must surrender to what is, and it will pull me through.

Please note that this stage is not spiritual bypassing. Spiritual bypassing is denying or avoiding unpleasant feelings and emotions, and instead feeling you can hide behind spiritual principles and rise above. This stage is not spiritual bypassing because of the work done in Stages 1-3, where you faced fears and listened to parts that weren't always pleasant (Fear, Doubt, Imposter, Self-Conscious Parts). You already heard the chatter and worked through it. Now they are a gentle reminder that you know the voices that will not serve you moving toward your dream. So, you nonchalantly disengage from the process of listening to the fears and keep your eye on the prize.

Child's Pose Representation

I'm not sure if I went into the child's pose when I had my cringe-and-crying moment. But I probably would have and I know I would have found comfort doing it, too.

> **Journal Prompt:** Write what words you would say to comfort the Part of you that just needs to surrender and pause when bumping up to the tests of this stage.

❋

The Divine Dream Dance

STAGE 6: COMPLETE DIVINE FLOW

"Being completely involved in an activity for its own sake. The ego falls away.
Time flies. Every action, movement, and thought follows inevitably from the
previous one, like playing jazz. Your whole being is involved, and you're using
your skills to the utmost."
~ Mihaly Csikszentmihalyi

Joy and ease help mark this stage. This stage is very similar to Stage 4. What is different is that the strength, confidence, and trust that you experienced from making it through Stage 5 brings you more firmly into this stage of wholeness, perfection, and completeness. Here, you are undisturbed by the Parts that can throw you off track, whereas, in Stage 4, you are a little more susceptible to those Parts. You know, without question, that the show must go on, and you keep moving forward. You feel empowered and liberated. You experience the joy and bliss of living the life of your dreams. You live life from your heart and not from the limiting stories.

You are vibrating high. Your mind supports your heart's desires. All of your Inner Parts are calm, balanced, and in harmony. Your Parts understand that this is your Divine Flow, and there is no need to question or doubt. You are one with your dream dance and one with the symphony of your dreams and purpose.

Not only are you not being mystified by the fear and attachment to an outcome, but you are also feeling detached from the Ego. The temptation to run or self-destruct from the Self-Sabotage Part is non-existent. You are not caught in some unrealistic expectation that is beyond human. You are suspended somewhere in between the world of thinking, *I am awful and can't do it,* and the world that is grandiose and putting pressure on you and your dream to be perfect. You are connected to the journey itself, the process, your calling. "Life's a journey, not a destination"—a lyric from an Aerosmith song. There is no definition of a specific outcome; you are not consumed by what people may think of your dream. You are entirely in the present moment of whatever step of your dream journey. This stage is fun and joyful.

Visual Representation

Dancer in the air. This image shows the ease, the ability to defy gravity. To be so completely in a place of trust that all you need is the air within and around you. Nothing needs seriousness or manipulation. Just dance!

Real Life Example

I knew I had reached this stage when it felt like everything between Stage 1 and Stage 6 collapsed. The knocking on my heart is the way. I don't have to question it or create barriers against it. That joy is what drives me. I am continuing to build a life that includes the expressions I feel passionately about on a daily basis. I feel connected and aligned almost all of the time. Not 100%, but almost. Sometimes I can get caught back on Stage 5, but the time there is shorter and less intense.

The best part is that the concern of what others will think has dropped away. That is not the focus. What people think of what I'm doing is NOT my North Star. My alignment to this joy, purpose, and Dharma is my joy. Of course, I hope that people will benefit from me following my dreams, but I do not get lost in that sauce.

If *one* person benefits from this book.

If *one* person benefits from my podcast.

If *one* person achieves their dreams after a transformation they experienced at one of my retreats.

Then, I am complete. And because I am *one* person that has benefited from all of the above. I am complete.

I will sing. I will write. I will dance. I will know and live my Big Dream and help others know and live theirs. I will illuminate the light within you and help you dissolve the stories blocking the way to your dreams.

Dancer in the Air Representation

Like the dancer leaping into the air, my life flows with so much more ease these days. Less resistance. Less stories holding me back and binding me.

Journal Prompt: Write a description of you living with ease, freedom, flow and joy. Allow whatever comes to you be what you write when you envision yourself defying the gravity of limiting beliefs and living out your fullest expression.

Final Thoughts about the *Divine Dream Dance*

1. Remember that you can move back and forth within the six stages. This will especially happen if you begin a "new dream." I have found that the foundation of Stages 1-3, if fully experienced, means that Stages 4-6 are smoother, and you don't always need to go back into Stages 1-3.

2. Stages 5 and 6 are not Spiritually Bypassing because of your work in Stages 1-3. These stages include being with and listening to your negative emotions. Spiritual Bypassing is when you skip and avoid any seemingly unpleasant or negative feelings or unresolved issues and cover and replace any of that with an ideal belief like, "Everything happens for a reason."

3. I know that if I do not follow the expressions of my heart, I will block my joy and purpose. I will be blocking my ability to help myself and others heal, learn, grow, connect, create, and boldly follow our dreams by illuminating and transforming the stories that bind us. I'm committed to working through these stages and overcoming the fear of being vulnerable whenever it comes up. I promise to help you do the same. That way, you, too, can be connected to song, joy, and your birthright to connect with music, regardless of what the inner and outer critics say.

CHAPTER 16

✳

The Opportunity *and* Space for You to Transform

"We cultivate love when we allow our most vulnerable and powerful parts of ourselves to be seen and known. When we honor the spiritual connection that grows from that offering with trust, respect, kindness and affection."
~Brené Brown

In Stage 3 of the Divine Dream Dance, I listed several ways to transform our stories, from mindfulness to psychotherapy to hypnosis and shamanic healing. For the remainder of this book, I have explicitly focused on creative, expressive, and performing arts. Giving everyone the opportunity and space to be vulnerable and creatively express themselves while being witnessed is the most empowering opportunity and tool we can offer to help people follow their dreams. Performing arts make us vulnerable, and vulnerability encourages connection. Witnessing others gently confront the stories that have kept them bound and then using the healing powers of music and other expressive arts is priceless. It is incredible to watch how music, nature, dance, and art are a shortcut to deep connections within ourselves, to each other, and to the divine wisdom.

Everyone has the right and permission to be imperfect while still being able to shine and do something they love. The final chapter of this book explains the power of using creative, expressive, and performing arts to conquer our fears, doubts, and other blocks to achieve joyous fulfillment in life. My mission is to ensure as many people as possible can experience the creative, supportive space and opportunity to break through binding stories that stand between them and their dreams.

Some words to help bring this belief home:

- "In many shamanic societies, if you came to a medicine person complaining of being disheartened, dispirited, or depressed, they would ask one of four questions: When did you stop dancing? When did you stop singing? When did you stop being enchanted by stories? When did you stop being comforted by the sweet territory of silence?" ~Gabrielle Roth

- Ancient Greek physicians and scholars like Hippocrates believed in treating the mind, the body, and the soul in a holistic way. One of the prescriptions they would give their sick patients was watching theatrical performances. This was not only for the "fun," but also for the mental, physical, emotional, and spiritual benefits they would experience as a result. Ancient Greece is the first finding that supports Art Therapy.

- Looking across history in every culture, creative and artistic expression has been used for survival,and healing. Slaves used them to endure the inhuman conditions they faced. Flamenco singing and dancing were born by the people in Southern Spain to express the grief of having spouses and family members ripped out from their arms and sent to another country because of their religion.

Though we can see it used all throughout history to help humans to connect and transform; survive and celebrate, we live in a time and society where most people are starving for creativity. In addition to history, brain science supports the power of creativity. Studies show it as a form of anti-anxiety and anti-depression. Creative, expressive and performing arts and their power resides in our history, our DNA and souls.

So, why aren't we all expressing ourselves creatively?

One theory as to why we aren't accessing the powerful modality of creative arts is because our Parts are carrying false stories that keep us from even attempting to incorporate arts and creativity into our lives in the simplest of ways. Let's illuminate these false stories here so that we can tame them and remove them as obstacles. By doing so, we open ourselves up to a world of fun, freedom, and fulfillment that creativity brings.

I'm not talented enough.

Has someone ever asked you to participate in an art form only to hear you respond with: "I can't do that?" When the truth is, you can. We can all sing, dance, draw, paint, and write to some extent. However, somewhere along the way, maybe a parent, teacher or mentor, with the best of intentions, told us that we weren't good at said art form and suggested we take up something else. We hear this false story from each other all of the time: "I can't draw. I can't sing, dance, paint…" (fill in the blank).

"We were all born creative" is something you will often hear from Dayna Wood of Integrative Counsel. She is a registered expressive arts therapist and also happens to be obsessed with brain science. When we do workshops together, she reminds our participants that our ancestors needed to be creative in order to survive. She follows up with the specific data and brain science that supports that notion. We had to be creative to survive as a species. Our brains are wired for creativity, and it's not just some woo-woo, warm and fuzzy notion.

Creativity is not a talent reserved for a select few, but a universal human trait. Therefore, we actually can sing, dance, paint, draw, etc and we just choose not to because we have a story that we carry that we need to be schooled or talented in order to perform. Infants and small children are a beautiful example of life before this story. Very soon after we come out of the womb we begin moving to a beat or humming to a melody. Eventually, children find natural joy in singing the alphabet or moving to the song "Head, Shoulders, Knees and Toes." Give a child crayons and a coloring book and they are captivated. What happens to us by the time we reach adulthood? Sadly, we have evolved into a society that has brought judgment of these artistic expressions to an extreme, so that if we weren't or aren't encouraged to continue using art forms or worse yet, told that we shouldn't, we stop and do not continue using them into adulthood.

Think of the most recent wedding you went to. Did the people on the dance floor sing and dance? Did they seem happy or miserable? Or the most recent time you witnessed karaoke. What was the general mood? Maybe you've been fortunate enough to attend a sip-and-paint or a pottery class. What was the overall feeling of people attending? I would bet your answer is not just "happy," but pure, unadulterated joy and a sense of connection that is hard to find in other activities.

Arts are self-indulgent.

Somewhere along the line, we have defined art as a luxury only those with time and wealth can afford to pursue. We've been told that we cannot make good money doing art, so we should not do it for that reason. Whether it's because we are supposed to be doing something more "industrious" or because it is a waste of time, it is heartbreaking to see the diminished prioritization of art and creativity. Interestingly enough, taking time to be creative helps us be more productive and imaginative and solve problems in ways far beyond what our logical, left brains can do.

We deserve not only to access art but also to make it a priority in our lives. In doing so, we experience the mental and physical benefits and access wisdom and answers we would not usually find. For example, writing a poem can help us find ourselves on the other side of grief or losing a relationship. A collage will help us understand what we truly want in life. Using images to help represent what we desire is called a vision board. The more we incorporate art and change the story about it being some form of luxury, the more we will discover that it is a necessity.

Author and one of my dearest friends, Hope Koppelman, has a passage in her book *The Gifts of Writing* that states:

> "Art is one of the most powerful and effective tools we have to transform the world, because of how quickly it can lead us from darkness to light, from confusion to clarity, from ugliness to beauty, from pain to healing... As long as we have art in the world, we will always have a pathway to light and clarity and beauty and healing."

The vulnerability of creative arts should be avoided.

Creativity is indeed vulnerable, but that does not mean we should avoid doing it. The power to heal, learn, and grow lies within and on the other side of that vulnerability. The ability to conquer loneliness, sadness, and disconnection happens because of that vulnerability. Author and researcher Brené Brown says it best:

> "We cultivate love when we allow our most vulnerable and powerful parts

of ourselves to be seen and known. When we honor the spiritual connection that grows from that offering with trust, respect, kindness, and affection."

It's true that it takes courage to be vulnerable, and avoidance is not the antidote. When we face our fears of vulnerability and allow ourselves to access creativity, we actually find unique and effective ways to transform whatever challenges we may be facing. Take music, for example. Ever use a song to help heal a heartache? Take that a step further and write your own song to empower yourself and give hope to whatever you are facing. The opportunities for healing and transformation are endless in the form of arts when you are courageous enough to step toward them and not let these false stories stop you.

FALSE STORY #4

I must listen to the inner and outer critics, and silence myself.

As you already read in Stage 4 of my personal experience of the Divine Dream Dance, when it comes to the vulnerability of artistic expression, we often encounter an Inner Critic Part dissuading us from wanting to practice creative expression. We cannot let this story get in the way of accessing the profound power of creative expression. Often, our Critic Parts think they are keeping us safe and protecting us. For example, there may be a fear of vulnerability and embarrassment in artistic expression, so critical efforts are there to prevent that from ever being a remote possibility. Despite their best intentions, critical parts within ourselves or from the Critic Parts of others can hinder experiencing the freedom and benefits of artistic and creative expression. Letting go and being able to express these innate artistic qualities born and residing within each of us opens us up to abundant inner resources of wisdom and innovation. When we can get our Critic Parts to step aside, the Artistic Parts within us can expand. Our Artistic Parts us open the door to our subconscious and unconscious, where there is depth and understanding beyond what our conscious mind can access.

The next time you notice one of the above stories getting in the way of you expressing yourself creatively, see it with curiosity and gentle compassion. That awareness will help put you in the driver's seat rather than the false story of driving the bus and blocking access to your innate creative necessities. When you can step forward and transform your life positively through the arts, you will access unlimited resources and find growth and expansiveness. Solutions around any obstacles or difficulties you are experiencing will appear in the most subtle and enjoyable ways. Transformation and evolution will occur. Just give it a try, and you will see.

Making Space for Creative Expression in Our Lives

This book's last section offers very natural and organic snapshots of my life that exhibit the many benefits of creative expression. These glimpses will start stirring something within you and help you recall times when you have experienced examples like this in your own lives.

Power of Creative Expression Example #1: It was around 2008 in Cambridge, MA. I am out dancing at a club called The Elephant. They played the best 90s dance music, and what made it even more special was it was the music that I danced to as an adolescent and in my early 20s, the ages that often determines the genres we prefer for the rest of our lives. Biggie Smalls, P-Diddy, my body is starting to move while I write this. I will never forget this gorgeous young lady (at the time, I was around 29 years old, and she was probably around 23 years old) who was watching me dance, and she said: "That looks like so much fun; I've never danced in public." Naturally, I responded: "Well, you are now!" I gestured for her to stand up and start dancing. I saw the joy and transformation on her face. In the next scene, she is moving, and it looks like complete euphoria. Why?? Dancing is in the fabric of our souls and our culture of being. She looked at me with tremendous gratitude and thanked me for encouraging her to dance in public.

Power of Creative Expression Example #2: I host regular karaoke parties. One of my absolute favorite parts of these parties is when people come to me afterward and say, "I've never done anything like that before; that felt great!" People send me emails days after about how liberating and connecting it is to sing like that. Why? Because we are born to sing.

Power of Creative Expression Example #3: When my niece Amber was a toddler, she hated being placed in the car seat and taking baths. So, I started to sing to her during these times; she would immediately soften, open, and start singing with me. She immediately forgot all the resistance and protest she had prior. Why? Music is a language that cuts through all logic and defenses.

Power of Creative Expression Example #4: Whenever I facilitate or attend a creative arts workshop where people draw, paint, or make collages, everyone immediately starts to connect. We start relating to one another like we are children, full of wonder, in our kindergarten class again. Why? Painting, drawing, art are in our bones.

Power of Creative Expression Example #5: I can still see myself in my bedroom as a teenager. One of my first crushes broke up with me. Suddenly Phil Collins comes on the radio singing *Against All Odds* and I sing and acknowledge the poetic lyrics. Suddenly, I feel heard, validated and understood. The lyrics combined with song and melody soothes the soul.

Together, we could fill pages with examples. Poetry, drama, drawing, painting, writing, singing, dancing, photography, crafting, cooking—I consider all of these creative expressions, all of this art, and all of this the most healing and transformative tools at our fingertips.

One final request: Commit to opportunities that give you the space and resources to use creative and expressive arts to transform your stories. Whether you carve out time in your schedule to do it alone or you go to something structured like a workshop or a retreat, give yourself this gift. Check out *www. thewowretreat.com*, and if being in a supported group calls to you, I will see you there!

> **Journal Prompt:** Write 3 ways you plan to incorporate Creative Expression into your life in the next 30 days. Anything from singing in the shower, joining a dance class or going to a writer's retreat. The opportunities are endless. Write down the first 3 that come to your mind and commit to making it happen.

And remember: *you own the story*. Follow your joy. Make your dream a reality.

"If you own the story, you get to write the ending."
~ Carl Jung

Acknowledgments

A special thank you to my husband, Andy Lutts, for your steadfast, consistent, and unconditional love swirled with your "no-doubt". You have helped me heal and break through the stories between me, us, the WOW STAGE, and writing this book. You did countless edits and allowed me to bounce off idea after idea after idea. You are my rock. The fact that you have written two books inspired me too. I love you to infinity, you special man.

My clients and retreat participants, past and present: you need to know how much you enrich my life. The pleasure and honor that you chose me to copilot your journey is beyond describable. Healing, learning, growing, creating, and connecting together is a dream come true for me. Now, let's make your dreams a reality and have fun while we're doing it!

The WOW STAGE Team—thank you for helping make my dreams a reality. Mick and Tess Pulver. Shannon Ward and Leilane Kane. Cassidy, Dallas and Matthew Brooks-Bowling, and Alli Cravener. Michelle Gallant. Ogechukwu Ogbonna. Prin. Jackie DelVecchio and Dayna Wood.

My dear friend/sister, Kelly Cherry, who accompanied me with guitar when I sang at The WOW STAGE, cheered me on and gently nudged me forward. And her husband Fred Cherry for helping out at The WOW STAGE by being the light he is.

My dear coven of Dayna Wood, Hope Koppleman and Camille Bianco. You are always cheering me on and reflecting spiritual depth, love, wonder, and possibility.

Rita Landy: thank you for believing in me, the WOW mission, and this book and all the people it could help. Thank you for listening to me talk about it and letting me test concepts out on you, too!

My therapists, coaches, and healers (all listed below under Resources with their contact info).

My developmental editor, Mary Bergida DeLuca, who took this book to new levels and helped this book expand while expanding me as a writer in the most gentle, intuitive, and powerful ways. You are the best! Thank you to Lauren Sapala for connecting us. I will forever be grateful.

First readers: Karen Frasca and Megan McIntire, who so eagerly agreed to be the first readers of my finished book before going off to editing. You both inspire me to expand in your own unique ways.

My editor: Timothy Lutts, who is also my beloved brother-in-law, edited this book with gentleness, precision and encouragement. An incredible combination for a difficult role.

My book designer, Kate Reingold: You took these pages and made them look crisp, clear and professional with such joy, patience, diligence and enthusiasm. All under a strict deadline for my WOW Retreat.

My cover (front and back) illustrator, Noah Stevens: You are truly an old soul and well beyond your years. I love how I give you a vision and you bring it to life with such ease. So grateful I stumbled upon you at Windhover.

My professional mentors: Marianne Williamson, Brené Brown, Richard Schwartz, Wayne Dyer, Byron Katie—I stand on the shoulders of giants who came before me to write these thoughts and ideas.

To all my friends and family that I may not have listed here. It's hard to include everyone. I know how fortunate I am to be held in the hearts of so many people. I love you and I thank you. You all have a patch in my quilt.

Appendix

List *of* Common Stories

Many thanks to all of the participants and other people who have volunteered and shared their stories so that we can set free as many people as possible.

Life in General

Nothing comes easy.

Couples/Romance/Love

You don't appreciate all that I do.
I'm not pretty, smart, or interesting enough to be loved.
I'm too fat to date anyone.
I am broken, so nobody will ever want to be with me.
If I can't change you, there's something wrong with me.
Because I have been duped in a relationship before, I will be duped again.
If I commit to someone, I will hurt them, so I'll just stay single.
My divorce taught me that there is no such thing as happy endings.

Money/Work

I have to work hard to make money.
I have to work all of the time so that I'm never homeless.

Family/Parenting

Everything has to be perfect for my kids, otherwise, I'm a neglectful parent.
I owe my parents so much because I treated them poorly.
I do not deserve a big home.

Self-Esteem/Body Image

I'm never going to lose weight because I let myself go for too long.

Giving and Receiving

If someone gives to me, they are expecting something in return.
It's a burden on someone else if I receive, so I will remain self-reliant.

Procrastination and Perfectionism

If it's not going to be perfect, I'm not even going to try to start or finish something.

Career/Success

My mental health challenges around OCD, anxiety, and depression make me feel like a failure, and unable to have the career and social life I used to have.
I am aging out of my profession because of rapid technology advancements.
If I celebrate my successes, I will be punished for being self-righteous. I must stay humble.

Mental Health/Mental Wellness

When my heart races and my chest tightens, I think it's a heart attack when it's actually anxiety.

Grief

I don't have a right to grieve that person because I am not immediate family. It's harder on them than me.
If I am not sad, that means I do not care.
If I let go of the grief (anger, sadness, etc.), I let go of the memory of the person.

Creative Arts

I'm not good enough to sing, paint, dance, etc.
Arts are self-indulgent.

Parts *and* Definitions

This section is to help further define the classification of parts that we find in our Internal Family System. I always encourage clients to find and discover their own name for their Parts. However, these classifications and examples are really helpful in making sense of our inner world.

Note: All of our Parts are valuable, sacred beings with talents and unique qualities to help keep our system in balance as best they know they can. Trauma and attachment forces them out of their natural state (*taken from a training with Dr. Schwartz).

Common Parts in Internal Family Systems

In addition to some of my observations and identification of Parts, I collected and implemented these definitions from the following resources including:
- *http://sfhelp.org/gwc/IF/strategies.htm*
- *https://www.seancuthbert.com/post/types-of-inner-critic-in-internal-family-systems-ifs-therapy*
- Holmes, Tom (2007). *Parts Work An Illustrated Guide to Your Inner Life.*

Part	Definition
Self	The Core of Our Being. Characterized by mindful awareness, compassionate connectedness, calm, confidence, clarity, creativity, curiosity and courage. A palpable peace available to all of us. Able to observe the other parts for a place with these qualities.
Manager Parts	These protector parts assess our needs and capacities and develop as a way to help manage internal and external demands (multi-tasker, scheduler, delegator, perfectionists, people pleasers, care-takers, fixer, martyr, OCD are some of the many examples).

Part	Definition
Firefighter Parts	These protector Parts are impulsive and reactive and literally try to fight the flames of the emotions of our exiles by extinguishing them. Food, sex, alcohol, drugs, work, and addictions that help distract you and numb your emotions. Sometimes Rage or Fight/Flight can be a Firefighter. Biggest Firefighter is suicide. Often trying to protect the exile of shame and criticism.
Exiles	Abandoned parts of ourselves. When we encounter a dysfunctional family dynamic or trauma or attachment challenges, we end up abandoning the part that is carrying the pain and hurting from a particular experience. We ignore them. Hide and lock them away somewhere deep within. These are often young and vulnerable parts of ourselves. Often carry shame and criticism.
Saboteur Parts	Causes covert trouble for someone for a good cause. These parts focus on interfering when something is going well in an effort to do what they think is protection. Procrastination Part, Doubt Parts, What if Parts. Defensive Parts. Destroyer (attacks your self-worth). Imposter Part, Social Anxiety Part, and Paranoid Part.
Inner Critic Parts	These parts try to protect you from the judgment of others. Some specific parts may be named: Perfectionist, Inner Controller, Underminer, Guilt Tripper.
People-Pleaser Parts	These parts want to be loved, accepted and keep the peace and harmony. Conformist (wants you to be part of a group).
Fixer Parts	Similar to People Pleasing Part, these parts are trying to make everything okay. They may be called the Problem Solver Part or Caretaker Part

Agreements *and* Listening/Speaking Skills

Before sharing your Layers of Stories Technique with each other, review these agreements and listening and speaking skills to help guide your healing conversation in a safe and productive way.

Agreements

We agree:
- That the goal of this is not to blame, point fingers or determine who is right and who is wrong – the goal of this is to allow each person to illuminate and voice the stories that are contributing to this conflict so they can be seen and healed
- To take each person's concerns seriously and use humor appropriately
- That I do not need to be defensive and judge myself or the other person, I just need to be present, with curiosity and compassion around what the other person is experiencing
- To see each other as equal partners trying to heal, learn and grow individually and together
- To practice non-judgment and compassion toward self and each other in whatever phase of the process you are in and whatever part or story is coming up for you. Keep in mind that this is not linear and will change for each of you. You could be in one phase one week and a different phase another week.
- To be open to the gray as most things won't be black and white. Two opposing things can be true at the same time. (e.g. you love each other **and** you have resentment)
- To practice active listening skills and effective speaking skills, including (I- statements)
- That we are committed to trying to lead from your authentic Self in this process (versus leading from a part such as grief, anger, guilt, etc.). Commitment to learning the art of speaking for a part, not from the part
- That we can trust the process and see it to completion

What else will you need in order to feel safe and supported in this process?

Strategies for the Listener

I recommend you set a time and take turns with these roles. Begin by setting the timer for 15 minutes each. So, for 15 minutes, one person is the Listener and practices these listening strategies while the other person speaks. Then switch roles for 15 minutes.

1. Show you're listening attentively with your body language (open your posture toward them, eye contact)
2. Accept silence.
3. Clarify what you hear. Ask open ended questions like what and how versus why.
4. Reflect what you hear. Whether you simply parrot back exactly what they said or take it a step further and offer empathy (e.g. If I were in your shoes, I would've felt....)
5. Confirm with the speaker that your reflection was accurate and they felt heard.
6. Ask if they need anything else (apology, explanation, etc.)

    Note: heated discussions often trigger us to go on the defensive. However, when we get defensive and speak from that Defensive Part, it can discount anything the listener shared. This not only leaves them feeling unheard, but the conversation has derailed and it's no longer constructive and effective. I highly recommend you ask your defensive part to step aside during this conversation

Strategies for the Speaker

1. Speak attentively. Face the listener and speak clearly and directly without being harsh.
2. Use I statements. Avoid you statements and blaming instead say: I feel _____ (basic feeling words: hurt, sad, scared, angry) when you _____(very specific behavior). I wish you would

    _____.
3. Be concise. Try to stay on topic.
4. Take a breath.
5. Avoid cross examination.
6. Check in for reflections to ensure you are speaking clearly and effectively and getting your point across.

Note-Taking Page

Use this to help organize your thoughts and keep track of what you hope to take away and integrate from this book. No more dog tags or trying to aimlessly find the page. It will all be here and organized for those of us that are visual learners.

I got this idea from Brené Brown's 10th Anniversary Edition of *The Gifts of Imperfection*. She got the idea from Maria Popova's Alternative Indexing Approach.

Idea	Page # or Time Stamp	Notes
Favorite Quotes		
Favorite Lessons		

Idea	Page # or Time Stamp	Notes
Stories You Can Relate To		
Want to Read/Learn More		
Didn't Understand		
Want to Share This		

Idea	Page # or Time Stamp	Notes
Had No Idea		
Hard to Hear This		

Resources

These are the coaches, healers and teachers that helped me along the way:

- Christa Pfeiffer, Voice Coach: _www.christapfeiffer.com_

- Dayna Wood and her Integrative Counsel Team Therapists:_ www.inte-grativecounsel.com_

- Elizabeth Tener, Therapist, LICSW (She has since retired.)

- J.P. Horgan, Transformational Coach: _https://thenextstepsacademy.com_

- Kira Pullig, Therapist, LICSW: _www.kirajpullig.com_

- Kelly Russell, Life/A Course in Miracles Coach: _www.rockyourjoy.com_

- Lisa Desrosiers, Shamanic Healer: _www.davissquareacupuncture.com_

- Michelle Gallant:_https://heartofblissdotco.wordpress.com/classes-and-events_

- Mick and Tess Pulver, Music Coaches: mick@bigembrace.com

- Dr. Richard Schwartz, Founder of Internal Family Systems: _https://ifs-institute.com/_

To sign up to be a part of the _Illuminating the Stories That Bind Us_ podcast, go to _www.jenniferhcarey.com/podcasts_.

References

Brown, B. (2012). *Daring Greatly: How the Courage to Be Vulnerable Transforms the Way We Live, Love, Parent, and Lead.* Penguin Random House Audio Publishing Group.

Brown, B., Fortgang, L. (2015). *The Gifts of Imperfection.* Hazelden Publishing.

Bauer, D. (2015). *One of America's Most Beloved Authors Just Told us Her 'Number One Life Hack' for Lasting Relationships.* www.businessinsider.com.

Chopra, D. (2017). *The Seven Spiritual Laws of Success: A Practical Guide to the Fulfillment of Your Dreams.* Hay House Publishers Pvt. Ltd.

Dispenza, J. (2018). *Breaking the Habit of Being yourself: How to Lose Your Mind and Create a New One.* Hay House

Eger, Edith E. (2017). *The Choice.* Simon and Schuster. Pg. 17

Greer, Carl. (2014). *Change Your Story, Change Your Life: Using Shamanic and Jungian Tools to Achieve Personal Transformation.* Findhorn Press.

Hendricks, Gay. (2009). *The Big Leap. Conquer Your Fear and Take Life to the Next Level.*

Hotchkiss, Sean. (2020). *How to Change your Story.* Men's Health Magazine, pages 64-65.

Koppleman, Hope. (2020). *The Gifts of Writing: Exploring the Mystery, Magic and Wonder of the Creative Process.* Hk Publishing Inc.

Katie, B. Katz, M. (2006). *I Need Your Love—Is That True?: How to Stop Seeking Love, Approval, and Appreciation and Start Finding Them Instead.* Three Rivers Press.

Pueblo, Yung. (2023). *The Way Forward.* Andrew McMeel Publishing.

Schwartz, Richard. (2023). *No Bad Parts: Healing Trauma and Restoring Wholeness with the Internal Family Systems Model.* Ebury Publishing.

Viskontas, I. (2019). *How Music Can Make You Better.* Chronicle Books.

http://www.mysahana.org/biology-of-forgiveness/

Made in the USA
Middletown, DE
29 August 2024

59836974R00108